MW00882680

Quadcopters and Drones

A Beginner's Guide to Successfully Flying and Choosing
the Right Drone

By Mark Smith

ISBN-13: 978-1514708422
ISBN-10: 1514708426
Quadcopters and Drones: A Beginner's Guide to Successfully Flying and Choosing
the Right Drone

Table of Contents

Introduction

Have you ever wanted to get a bird's eye view of the world around you? Have you ever wondered what our fascinating planet must look like through the eyes of an eagle as it soars effortlessly through the big blue skies? Yeah, me too and guess what? Me and you or you and I (*Grandma always said proper English was important)* are not the only ones itching to fly either.

Just about every person has wondered or even dreamed about what it must be like to fly. I can remember specific dreams where all I had to do was jump three times to fly. The first jump was your average normal jump. Not being the athletic type, this meant the first jump would launch me a few inches from the ground.

The second jump would get me a little further from the ground, but nothing truly breathtaking. The third jump though, that was when things got crazy. That third jump would break the force of gravity and send me screaming through the air like a jet.

Of course, when the dream ended I awoke with a huge smile on my face but was inevitably grounded just like every other person on the planet. The euphoric rush of flying was short lived and I always wanted just a few seconds more.

The reality is simple. We are not built to fly. I have yet to meet a person who has the natural ability to fly. Do you know anyone with wings? I sure don't. That leaves us humans with very few flying options.

Airplanes, helicopters, gliders, ultralights, jet packs and the good old lawn mower engine welded to an industrial sized fan blade that straps to your back using nothing more than Velcro. I don't know about you, but I am not strapping a lawn mower engine with a large industrial sized fan blade to my back. Nope, not going to happen.

That leaves airplanes, helicopters, gliders, ultralights and jet packs and unfortunately very few of us have our own private jet, helicopter or glider sitting on some secret launch pad high atop the Swiss Alps. Who can afford those types of toys anyways? I know I can't, and neither can anyone I know. Maybe I am just socializing with the wrong people.

Just five short years ago, if I was to tell you there was an easier, more affordable way to get your flying fix while keeping your feet firmly planted on the ground; you and everyone else would laugh and say I was crazy. Heck, there are people who still do that today but that's what happens when I go outside wearing a clown suit.

All joking aside, technology has now made it possible for you and I to finally get our flying fix without owning a jet, helicopter, glider or a jet pack. And just completely forget about the whole lawn mower engine industrial fan blade thing.

For the cost of your average meal at a nice restaurant, you could be flying a drone, and let me tell you a little secret. Flying one of these aerial machines is totally awesome. From the small nano-drones, to the mutli-engine hexacopters that allow you to strap a high definition 4k camera to a completely stable 3-axis gimbal in order to see everything in real time, and capture the footage in glorious high definition as you fly your eye in the sky is nothing short of a technological miracle. Not to mention, it is an adrenaline rush filled experience like none other.

Yes, there are drones that magically beam a live camera feed right back to you on the ground with next to no lag or latency in the video feed. That bird's eye view is finally yours. Think about that for second. Talk about getting a different perspective on things, this is it my friend! You have the ability to fly!

Why Do You Want to Fly?

We all want to fly for the same basic reason. Because it is fun, but knowing the honest answer to this question could save you a lot of time, frustration and money. Here's why. There are several very different drones on the market today. These drones range in price, size, technological advances and designed usage.

When I say "designed usage," I simply mean some drones are designed with a specific purpose in mind. They all fly and that is a huge part of the attraction here, but some of these flying machines can race across the sky at speeds exceeding 80 miles per hour or 128 kilometers per hour.

Would this be the right drone for a newbie who is looking to get off the ground? Of course not. In fact, choosing a racing drone as your very first flying machine would be a disastrous mistake that could very well end up with someone getting seriously hurt. Think your first drone purchase through. This is one hobby where fools and their money are soon parted or even hurt.

Knowing what you want to get from your flying experience will help you choose the right flying machine the first time. There are drones designed for aerial photography, FPV flying (first person view), racing, long distance flights and the general hobbyist. Don't worry, I will cover each type of drone in more detail a little later in this book.

The initial idea here is to go outside and have fun. Don't over complicate things by getting a flying machine with too many buttons, options or features. Some of these flying machines are extremely high tech and if you are not the type that easily fits into modern technology, then owning a fancy drone with all the bells and whistles might not be for you.

Remember, these things go in the air and when you make a mistake be it a tree, a power line or a herd of cattle, your drone will come crashing to the ground in multiple pieces. Gravity is unforgiving and so is an impact with the ground from as little as 10 feet or 3 meters in the air.

You will crash your drone. It is not a matter of if, but a matter of when it happens. I don't say this to discourage you. I am telling you the truth because I would hate for anyone to spend a lot of money on a drone only to have it fall from the sky like a lead balloon.

BOOM! Your investment is now in pieces and you may or may not have tears streaming from your eyes as you clutch what is left of your high dollar flying machine in your trembling hands.

Your first drone should be simple, easy to use and come with a relatively small price tag unless of course you don't mind throwing your money away, and if that's the case I have some great beach front property for sale in Nevada. Email me for more info!

My First Time Flying

It didn't take much convincing for me to want to fly a drone. Before I even had a controller in my hand, I knew it was something I would really enjoy. The main attraction for me was the ability to record high definition video and take photographs from a different perspective.

I would finally be able to see the world just like a bird, but I wasn't going to jump headfirst into flying until I had a better understanding of everything involved. I didn't want to spend a thousand bucks on a drone only to see it magically fly away or come crashing to the ground. I needed to feel secure before I could shell out that kind of money.

You might feel the same way. That's what this book is for. It is here to help you choose the right drone and most importantly, how to safely fly the thing without crashing!

I decided to start out small and I would highly suggest you do the same. I purchased two small nanodrones from

Amazon for about $20.00 each. I could give one drone to my kids and I could pilot the other.

I figured we could learn how to fly together and maybe we could even start some type of drone wars around the house. I'm sure my wife would love to have one of these tiny little flying machines come crashing down on her head. I wonder how badly it would get tangled in her hair. Let's not find out.

The drones arrived in two days thanks to Amazon Prime.

As soon as they arrived I realized my first mistake. I only

ordered two drones. I have two children. The idea of them sharing one drone was not going to work out. I should have ordered three of them, but oh well.

I quickly read over the included instructions and realized there wasn't much to the controls. Two sticks controlled the basic movements of this tiny flying machine. The nanodrones didn't have any fancy GPS flight controllers built in. This was just a basic fly around for a few minutes type of drone. Again, this was an experiment to see if I could grasp the basics.

Once the drones were charged we headed outside. I didn't want the kids to crash the drones in the house and I didn't want my dogs to try and eat the things either not to mention the whole crashing into my wife's hair scenario. Outside it was!

It was time for our maiden voyage. It was time to put technology to work and fly like an eagle or in this case fly like a small dragonfly. I pushed the left stick up and the drone took flight. I let go of the stick and it just hovered there like a hummingbird. It's tiny little LED lights winked at me. I was amazed and I had not flown this nanodrone more than a few feet or a meter from the ground. I laughed out loud and said to my kids, "Hey, look at this thing fly!"

I was so entranced by this tiny flying machine that I didn't notice my kids were flying their little drone around the yard like it was a bat out of hell. Meanwhile, mine just floated and hovered there.

"Hey dad look at this. It can do flips!" yells my son as the drone he was piloting did somersaults through the air. Kids seem to take to technology so quickly. It took my kids all of five seconds to learn they could throw the drone high into the air and fly it immediately after it started to fall back to the ground. Like I said, kids are quick with these gadgets but they are also more careless.

My son decided to see how high he could fly this little drone. He flew beyond the range of the controller and the drone quickly came crashing down to the ground. Did it survive the crash? What do you think? There it was in pieces. Meanwhile, my drone was still gently hovering like a hummingbird just a few feet from the ground.

I was amazed. I slowly maneuvered the little drone around the yard for a little while until finally landing it perfectly on the sidewalk. Yes, I was hooked and yes I was ready for the next level. I spent the next two weeks flying my nanodrone around the front yard. I knew this little flying machine pretty well. It was time to buy a real drone.

Buying Your First Drone

This is most likely going to be the most difficult part about the entire drone hobby. There are several drones on the market out there and they come with a wide variety of options and price tags. I spent about two weeks bouncing back and forth trying to decide which drone would be right for me.

Every single time I would settle on a specific model, I would learn something about it that would prevent me from buying. Some models had bad reviews and some users were reporting random fly aways with specific models. Other models had specific elevation limits and I was planning on flying my drone from elevations of around 8000 to 10000 feet. That's 2438 or 3048 meters.

I was learning that it was very difficult to find the perfect drone that would do everything I wanted. You might be in the same exact situation right now.

After bouncing back and forth for weeks, I finally narrowed down my decision to two very different drones. One drone came in a kit that would require me to put every little piece together. The other drone would arrive RTF or ready to fly right out of the box. Both drones cost about the same amount of money too.

I was at a crossroads. I wanted to fly but I also wanted a better understanding of how my drone worked. I ultimately decided to go for the drone that came in a kit.

This might not be the right choice for you and I will cover the pros and cons I personally experienced in the next chapter. I will also go over the major brands and types of drones in an upcoming chapter as well. This information should help you narrow down your choices to one or just a couple of drone candidates.

The best advice I can give you is this. Do not go out and buy an expensive drone first. Buy a smaller one and spend plenty of time practicing your flight skills before you take the plunge. Go out far away from people and pilot your new flying machine in plenty of wide open spaces.

This first drone is nothing more than your training wheels. You will be getting a feel for how well or how difficult it is to fly this little monster and I can tell you from personal experience, the smaller nanodrones are much more difficult to fly. Once you become comfortable flying, get rid of the training wheels and set your sights on something better!

The main points to consider before buying your drone are:

- Price

- Ease of Use
- Controls
- Flight Time
- Camera Ability
- Flight Modes
- Durability and availability of spare parts.

To Build or Buy RTF, That Is the Question

Determining the answer to this question will really depend on what type of person you are. If you are the type of person who wants instant gratification, then a KIT drone most definitely is not the right choice for you.

Me personally, I like to tinker with things. I like to know what makes them work. This is just one reason why I decided to go with a drone that required assembly. There are a few other excellent reasons to build your own drone.

Learn How Your Drone Works

By building a drone from a kit, you will have a better understanding of how this thing works. You will know what each little part and piece does. This can really come in handy when something goes wrong. If for some reason your drone won't fly, you should be able to determine exactly why it is not flying because you put the entire thing together.

Easy Repairs and Replacement Parts

There is another great benefit to building your own drone. When you crash your drone and it breaks (Notice how I said when, not if?) you will know exactly which pieces need to be replaced. You will also find replacement parts much easier to find when compared to a RTF drone. Replacement parts are also much cheaper too!

RTF drones are not necessarily meant to be repaired when they break, at least not by you. When you crash a RTF drone and it breaks, you will have to send the entire drone in for repairs.

In most cases you will need to box up the entire drone and send it off to the manufacturer. If you happen to live in a foreign country or a country where there is no local manufacturer, then you will be shelling out a lot of money in shipping costs to have your RTF drone repaired.

You will also be expected to pay for the repairs if the crash was your fault. These repairs will cost much more than a few simple replacement parts. That is a pretty big advantage if you ask me, but like I said, building a drone from a kit is not for everybody.

Upgrades Are Easier

Depending on which drone kit you buy, you will quickly learn that upgrading your kit drone is much easier too. Here is an example for you. My kit drone is a DJI Flamewheel 450. It is a basic quadcopter. It has four props, four motors, and four ESCs which are all mounted on four independent arms.

Now if I wanted to upgrade my quadcopter to a hexacopter, I would only need to buy a few pieces. If I had purchased a RTF quadcopter and wanted to upgrade it to a hexacopter, guess what? I would have to buy an entirely new drone! We are talking quite a huge difference in cost here.

Most RTF drones can't be upgraded at all. They are meant to be flown as is. If you want more, then the manufacturer wants you to buy an entire new flying machine. The manufacturers are not being greedy. They are just operating a smart business.

I could also very easily add a myriad of accessories to my kit drone. I can change cameras, transmitters, batteries, motors, props, add landing gear or turn the thing into an insanely fast racing quadcopter. Doing this with a RTF drone will require some serious modifications and most likely void your warranty.

Battery Choices

With a kit drone you have a huge amount of choices for how you want to power your newly built flying machine. There are different manufacturers and power options which I will go over in a later chapter. The upside is the ability to choose your batteries and chargers.

There is another upside as well. Batteries for kit drones are usually much, much cheaper. You may be able to purchase three kit drone batteries for the price of one RTF drone battery and these batteries are pretty much made from the same materials. The higher priced RTF drone batteries and just one way the RTF drone manufacturers are able to keep their RTF drone costs down.

Software

Some kit drones will require you to install some software on your computer. You will then be able to plug your drone into the computer and make changes to the way some of the electronic components work. You can also apply firmware updates through this software as well.

Was It Easy to Assemble?

Here comes the biggest cons to building your own drone. Putting the thing together was not easy, not even slightly easy. There were a lot of different parts from different manufacturers and no real instructions on making them all work nicely together.

Putting the basic quadcopter together wasn't too difficult. A few tiny hex screws here, some double sided tape there. Soldering this wire here and that wire there. Burning my fingers and the occasional splash of molten solder on my legs was just part of the process. You know what they say, "No pain, no gain!"

A few short hours later and bam I had the shell of a quadcopter sitting on my dining room table. I stood back and marveled at my creation. It wasn't alive yet, but soon, real soon!

Adding the gimbal, the FPV camera, the transmitter and remote control, was not so easy. It was tough to say the least and the building process did bring out a few choice four letter words on more than one occasion. I struggled through it with a nice cold beer at my side. The beer helped bury those fancy four letters words that kept managing to cross my lips.

Finally! It was completed and I had a freshly charged battery. The moment of triumph was at hand. I eagerly went out front and walked to a nearby field. I was ready. I powered every thing up and let all the fancy gadgets go through their individual warm routines. I had a Home Point locked and a great GPS signal. I was ready to fly!

I pushed up on the left stick and all four engines spun

faster and faster and faster. Man this thing is loud, I said to myself over the humming engines. I pushed the left stick up even more and the drone got even louder but it wasn't taking off. Something wasn't right. It appeared to be pushing itself towards the ground not up into the sky.

It was then that I realized I had installed the props incorrectly. Two props are supposed to spin clockwise and the other two are supposed to spin counter clockwise. I knew this, but somehow during one of my many four letter word outbursts, I had managed to mix up the props. Instead of getting lift, my drone was doing the exact opposite. It was pushing itself down towards the ground. Stupid mistake on my part but an easy fix.

With the props properly installed, my drone took off like a rocket. I couldn't believe how easy it was to fly. Oh yeah, I was hooked!

Another Downside to Building Your Own Drone
There is yet another downside to building your own drone. You and only you are 100% responsible for how it works. If you mess something up and your newly built drone comes crashing to the ground or it doesn't even get in the sky, then it is up to you to find out why. There will not be anyone there to hold your hand and walk you through your new problem.

Yes, you can research your problem on the Internet. You might find an answer and you might not. It all depends on how good you are at researching things on the Internet. If you purchase a drone kit that is not very popular, I can almost guarantee things will be tough for you. Like I said, building a drone from a kit is not for everyone.

Should You Buy A RTF Drone?

Most people will choose a RTF drone over a kit drone any day of the week and there is good reason for this. When you choose a RTF drone, everything comes assembled and ready to fly. That's what the RTF stands for, remember? You will be able to enjoy almost instant gratification. I say almost because you will still need to charge up some batteries before you can fly.

Instructions! What A Concept!
When you order a RTF drone, you will most likely get access to some very extensive instructions. Don't toss these aside and immediately try to fly your drone. The more common drones by DJI, 3DR and other manufacturers are high tech pieces of equipment. I highly suggest you read every single word in the instruction manual and then read it again. Pound the information into your brain before you even attempt to fly.

Easy to Locate Firmware Updates

You should know by now that consumer hobby drones are loaded with some pretty crazy technology. The companies who make these consumer drones are always fine tuning and tweaking their products.

You can easily get your hands on these tweaks and updates too. Not to say that kit drones don't offer updates because they do, but your kit drone might consist of 3-4 different parts from 3-4 different manufacturers like mine did. Hunting for updates from all the different manufacturers can be a pain in the butt. With a RTF drone all of these updates are easy to find and apply to your RTF machine.

Fine Tuned Machines

The mass market consumer RTF drones are also extremely fine tuned to make it easier for you to fly from day one. With the kit drone, you will be required to do all the fine tuning. If this is your first drone, fine tuning how it flies may not be your idea of a good time.

Larger Community

There is also a much larger community that you can interact with when you buy a RTF drone. There are online forums where you can find plenty of advice from other people who have the same exact drone as you. This can be a huge benefit when you have a problem. You will often find a solution to your problem much faster than if you were to try and contact the manufacturer.

There are communities for kit drones too, but they are nowhere near as large as the RTF drone communities.

More Warranty Options
You will have warranty options for both types of drones, but some RTF drones have better warranty options. For instance, the 3DR Solo drone is the first drone of its kind to offer a really powerful warranty which states, "If the flight logs show Solo was lost or damaged due to a system error, 3DR will immediately repair or replace not only the drone, but your gimbal and GoPro as well." You won't find this type of warranty in a kit drone.

Better Software
Both types of drones offer software that helps you pilot your drone better, take better pictures and video, fly specific GPS assisted routes and more, but the RTF drones have a more robust finely tuned software suite that is usually free with the purchase of the drone.

Don't get me wrong because you can still find plenty of great software for kit drones, but once again it will be up to you to do all the fine tuning and tweaking.

Everything You Need In One Package
With a RTF drone you get everything you need to fly in one nice package. You will get the drone, the remote control, a battery, a charger and some additional

accessories. This is a huge plus.

Should You Buy RTF or A Kit Drone?
By now you should have a pretty good idea of which type of drone is right for you. If you are not the type that likes to build things, then an RTF drone is right for you. If you are the type that loves to put things together and loves a good challenge, then a kit drone is for you.

You could also go with a ARTF or almost ready to fly drone. This type of drone will arrive partially assembled. It will be up to you to finish the assembly.

You could always get one of each and enjoy the best of both worlds. That's what I ended up doing. Once I got really comfortable flying my kit drone around the skies, I wanted to see what the other half of the drone world was like. I ordered a RTF drone, specifically the Phantom 3.

I love flying both of my drones and now I have a backup for that fateful day when one of them comes crashing down to the ground and breaks into a million pieces on impact.

Learning the Lingo

I will be using quite a few terms throughout this book that you may or may not be familiar with. This is one of those hobbies where knowing as much information as possible will ensure hours of constant fun and zero frustration. I highly suggest that you DO NOT skip this section. It will just make things easier for you once you are in the air.

By all means, if you consider yourself an aeronautics expert then feel free to skip this important information, but if you think the term LIPO refers to a very popular cosmetic surgery process where fat is sucked out of a person's butt cheeks, then you might want to keep reading.

Accelerometer – A marvel of modern technology that simply measures how fast something is moving in a given direction. Most modern smart phones have accelerometers and so do most of the drones on the market today.

Altitude – Not to be confused with elevation because they are two very different things. Altitude refers to the height of an aircraft in regards to its takeoff location. For instance, if you launch your drone in the state of Florida and you fly it at around 50 feet or 15 meters in the air, then the drone altitude is 50 feet or 15 meters.

If you launch the same drone in the state of Colorado from

a mountain elevation of 8000 feet or 2438 meters and fly it at around 50 feet or 15 meters in the air, then you are still flying at an altitude of 50 feet or 15 meters. The elevation of the area where you initially take off has nothing to do with the altitude you are currently flying.

At the time of this writing, it was illegal in the United States to fly a drone at an altitude of over 400 feet or 121 meters. You don't want to be the person that crashes their drone into a passenger jet which ultimately results in a fiery crash where people die. Respect the rules and the laws. Keep your drone at a safe operating altitude.

ARTF – ATRF is an acronym which stands for Almost Ready to Fly. It refers to a drone or model aircraft that is only partially assembled. It is up to you to finish the assembly. This is a great choice for people who like to tinker and build.

Autonomous – In the drone world the term autonomous refers to a drone being able to fly on its own without any interaction from a human being. Welcome to the future!

Elevation – Elevation refers to the height of an area above sea level. Higher elevations can really slow a person down. The air is thinner. The thin air has the same effect on drones. They have to work harder to fly at higher elevations. Some drones won't even operate above elevations of 8000 feet. If you are going to purchase one of the more expensive drones, then you might want to double check elevation limits with the manufacturer before you make a purchase.

At higher elevations, flight times are reduced. Remember this if you plan on flying at higher elevations.

ESC – ESC is yet another acronym that stands for electronic speed controller. The ESC determines the amount of power that goes to an electric engine. The total amount of ESCs in a drone will depend on the total amount of motors.

Flight Controller - You could think of the flight controller as the main brain of today's drones. Flight controllers are what makes some of the more expensive drones easier to fly.

Some of the better flight controllers are responsible for keeping drones level, giving you multiple flight modes, GPS functions and other autonomous features that make flying a drone as simple as pushing a button. The downside to flight controllers is this. When they malfunction so does your drone.

Fly Away – This is something no drone pilot wants. A fly away is when a drone suddenly and for no apparent reason flies away never to be seen again. This is usually the result of an improper home position lock, but high electromagnetic interference has also been known to cause this painful phenomenon.

Many pilots affix a small GPS locating device to their drones in case something like this happens or in case of a far away crash.

FPV - If you haven't already noticed, the world of drones is full of acronyms. FPV stands for first person view and when speaking of drones, FPV gives you the ability to see exactly what the drone sees in real time.

There are goggles on the market with high definition displays that connect your point of view to the same point of view the camera on the drone sees. You can also use a computer or tablet for the FPV experience, but the goggles work best. Talk about a really cool experience, FPV drone flying is it.

FOV – Yep, another handy acronym. FOV stands for field of view and it is more of a camera enthusiast term because it refers to the actual field of view a specific camera has. Some cameras have a very wide field of view. A wide field of view means there is more landscape in the picture. An extremely wide FOV creates a fisheye effect. This is the common effect seen on GoPro cameras.

A narrow FOV means there is less landscape in the picture and lacks that interesting fisheye effect.

Gimbal – A gimbal is a rather amazing piece of technology that allows an object to remain independent of the rotation of the item supporting it. For example, if you were on a large ocean ship and the ship was moving from side to side due to the ocean waves, you and everything else in the ship would also be moving with the waves. This is what causes seasickness.

If you could stuff your body into a gimbal, then your body would not be impacted by the crashing waves. The gimbal would keep your body stable.

In the drone world, a gimbal is used to keep a camera steady and smooth while you fly. The movement of the drone does not affect the movement of the camera.

Ground Control Station – Ground control stations have been used by the military for years. It puts the controls of an unmanned vehicle on the ground and in the hands of a human being.

A ground control station for consumer drones makes it easy to draw a flight path on a computer screen and launch a drone along this flight path using GPS sensors and satellites. All of the important flight information can be seen on a computer screen. Altitude, current location, flight paths, speed, battery status and much more.

GPS – GPS has become rather common. Smart phones use GPS and so do many of today's modern vehicles. Some of today's drones also use GPS to not only help them fly smooth and stable, but to also relay their location back to the pilot.

Gyroscope – Another little technological marvel. Gyroscopes in drones help them maintain orientation and steady flight.

Hexacopter – This is a multi-rotor helicopter. The "HEX" part of the word refers to a copter with six spinning blades.

Home Position – Also commonly referred to as Home Point. Home position is calculated by the internal GPS system. Home position would be the GPS coordinates of where the drone initially takes off. Some drones set this position automatically before takeoff.

IMU – Can you believe there is yet another acronym? IMU stands for inertial measurement unit. In drones, the IMU usually contains accelerometers and gyroscopes.

Lipo – Lipo is short for lithium-ion polymer. This is what most drone batteries are made from. It is a very volatile, very dangerous material if not handled correctly. I will cover this more in a later chapter.

LOS – LOS is an acronym for line of sight. In the drone world, line of sight means being able to physically see your drone at all times. If you can't see your drone, it is no longer in LOS or line of sight.

At the time of this writing, it was illegal to operate a drone in the United States past your Line of Sight.

OSD – Not to be confused with OCD. OSD stands for on screen display. If you are using an FPV system, a ground control station or some sort of visual monitoring device, the OSD would be referring to your on screen display.

Pitch – Pitch refers to the movement of the nose or back end of your drone. Adjusting the pitch makes the nose or back end of your drone tilt down or up. The image makes it easier to understand.

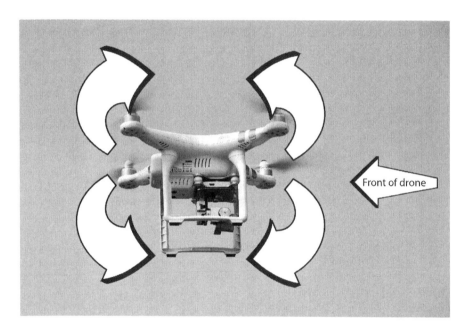

Front of drone

PMU – PMU stands for power management unit. It manages the power throughout your drone.

Octocopter - OCT means eight. In this case it refers to a drone with eight spinning blades.

Quadcopter – Quad means four. In this case it refers to a drone with four spinning blades. This is the most common configuration being used in consumer or hobbyist drones.

Receiver or RX – Drones are controlled by a transmitter, (the controller you hold in your hand) and the receiver. If you opt for a ready to fly drone, then you will most likely never see the receiver because it is located inside the drone itself. Its job is to receive the data from the controller and turn it into useful information that pilots the drone.

RTF – RTF stands for ready to fly. This a drone that arrives in a ready to fly condition. All you need to do is take it out of the box, read the instructions, charge the batteries and fly!

RTH – RTH stands for return to home. In some of the more consumer friendly drones, RTH is a fail safe mode that brings the drone back to where it took off from if it loses signal with the transmitter or if the pilot becomes disoriented with the direction the drone is currently flying. I like to call this my "Oh Shit!" button.

RTH can be activated with the touch of a button as long as a home point has been set by the GPS system located inside the drone. Most consumers drones will do this automatically as part of a pre-flight warm up routine.

Make sure your current home point is set to your current take off location. Many pilots forget this and when they activate the RTH feature, the drone will return to the last home point which was set. This could be miles away if the pilot has changed take off locations. This is the most common reason for fly aways.

Roll – A small piece of bread best served warm with a pat of butter. In the drone world, roll refers to the movement of you drone on a horizontal axis. Adjusting the roll will make the side of your drone tilt down or up. This image makes it easier to understand.

In this image the drone is facing the camera.

Spotter – A spotter is a second person whose job is maintaining line of sight at all times while the pilot focuses on their FPV. This is a good idea in case the FPV signal gets lost. The spotter will then be able to help the pilot visually locate the drone and fly it back home in case the RTH feature did not function.

Telemetry – All of the information being sent between the drone and the pilot's ground station.

Transmitter or TX – This is the remote control that you hold in your hand and use to control your drone.

UAV – UAV is an acronym for Unmanned Aerial Vehicle, a drone.

Waypoint – A location set by GPS within a flight path. Using a ground station gives you the ability to set several waypoints during your drone's flight path.

YAW – Yaw refers to the movement of your drone as it rotates in a circle. Adjusting the yaw with no forward movement will make your drone spin in a circle. This image makes it easier to understand.

This image was taken from below the drone looking up.

Congratulations! You are now educated on the many terms being used in the consumer drone market. You are one step closer to flying and a whole lot smarter than anyone who chose to not read this section! Let's take a closer look at a drone and what makes it function.

A Closer Look at the Kit Drone

Your basic kit drone will include hundreds of pieces but once everything is correctly assembled, you will have two main pieces. You will have the drone itself and the remote control. Let's take a closer look at the drone.

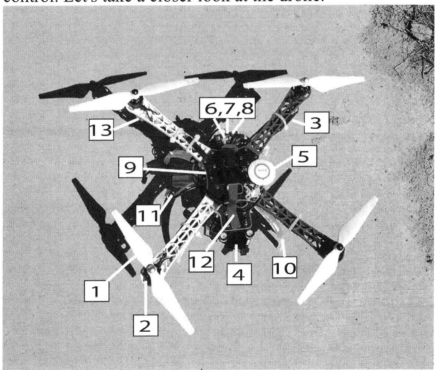

There is a lot going on in that picture up there. Let's take a closer look at all the pieces that make this kit drone fly.

1. These are the props or propeller. This is a

quadcopter so it has a total of four propellers.

2. Under each propeller is a motor. There is a total of four motors.
3. Attached to the arm is the ESC or electronic speed control. I already discussed what these do in the learning the lingo chapter. This is a quadcopter so there are four ESCs. One for each motor.
4. 3-axis camera gimbal. Notice there is no camera there? You must supply your own camera with this model. The preferred camera is a GoPro.
5. GPS / Compass Sensor.
6. Parts 6,7 and 8 are all located in the same area. Part #6 is the receiver. This is what receives the signal from the remote control.
7. Part #7 is the PMU. This routes power to all the pieces that require it.
8. Part #8 is the gimbal control unit. This controls the movement or tilt of the gimbal.
9. Underneath the top board is the flight controller. In this instance, the flight controller must be in the very center of the aircraft.
10. This is the landing gear.
11. This is the battery connector. This specific model uses a Deans connector.
12. Velcro battery strap. This is what keeps the Lipo battery in place.
13. This is the remote or status LED. By flashing a series of different colored lights, this little device

let's you know when your kit drone has acquired a home lock, a good GPS signal and an accurate nose position.

With a kit drone, you will be required to put all of these things together and ensure they are all functioning together as they should. All of these parts are easy to see, get to and change if need be. You will notice something entirely different on the RTF drone.

A Closer Look at the RTF Drone

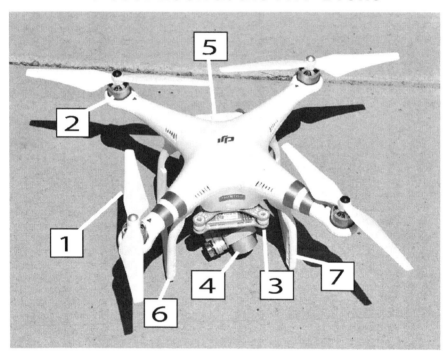

This is the very popular DJI Phantom 3 RTF quadcopter. The first difference you may notice is fewer parts. It has the same amount of parts but most of them are hidden underneath the top shell on the RTF drone. You don't have easy access to anything under the shell. Yes you can get in there, but not easily and you may very well void your warranty doing so. Let's take a closer look at the pieces that make it fly.

1. These are the props or propeller. This is a quadcopter so it has a total of four propellers.
2. Under each propeller is a motor. There is a total of four motors.
3. Camera gimbal. This keeps the image steady and as smooth as glass.
4. Included 4K camera. With the kit drone you will have to supply your own camera. This RTF drone comes with a 4K camera. The camera on this RTF model is fine tuned to this specific model. You have complete control over just about everything you could ever want or need. You can pan the camera from the remote control. You can see a live video feed of exactly what the camera sees. You can take a variety of different pictures. You can record glorious 4k high definition video and you can change things like shutter speed, ISO and frame rate. These are all very important in the world of photography.
5. Battery pack installed. This model features an intelligent battery that snaps into the body of the quadcopter.
6. This is the landing gear. The status LED lights are built into the landing gear on this model.
7. These are the status LED indicators. Two of them are bright red. This lets you know what part of the drone is the front. This can be really helpful when you are flying. Keeping things properly oriented is the best way to avoid a crash.

Where Are All the Other Parts?
All the other important parts like the GPS, IMU, PMU and flight controller are tucked away nicely under the top shell.

Now that you can clearly see the huge differences in the two types of drones, let's take a closer look at the two different remote controllers.

A Closer Look At the Kit Drone Remote Control

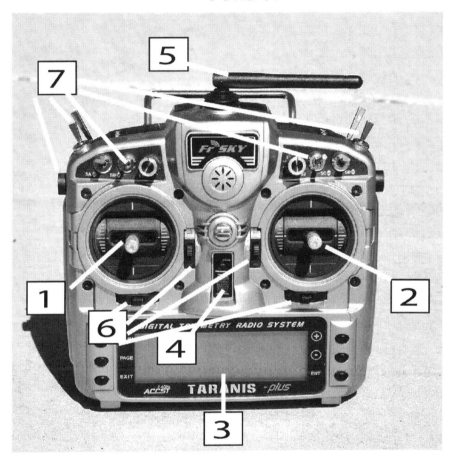

When I first laid eyes on this remote control, the very first thing that popped into my head was, "Wow! There are a lot of buttons on this thing. It looks very complicated." Most of the buttons and switches on this remote are user assigned to various functions on the drone. I only use a few of them myself.

1. This is the left control stick. I will cover more of what it actually does a little later in the book.
2. The right control stick.
3. This is the display screen. Some remote controls will display a live video feed from the drone right here. This one just gives me other important information.
4. This is the power switch.
5. This is the antenna.
6. These are the four trim switches. They allow you to fine tune the two different movements of each control stick.
7. The 30-40 other buttons that the pilot can assign to specific functions. For instance, I have assigned one rotating switch to tilt the gimbal. I have assigned another switch as my return to home switch. One flick of that switch and the drone will take over and hopefully fly back to the locked home position.

On the back of the remote is the battery compartment. This specific remote uses a small rechargeable battery pack. You just plug the controller into the wall and it charges the battery pack.

Another interesting thing to note about going with the kit drone is this. You will be required to choose the remote control. Some retailers will offer a bundle that includes a controller, others will not. You will also be responsible for binding or assigning all of the stick and button functions to the drone.

Through software you set each control stick or button to a specific function of the drone. This gives you complete and total freedom on how and what the remote controller makes the drone do. This can be good and bad. The good part is having complete and total control. The bad part is trying to figure out how to bind everything!

A Closer Look At the RTF Drone Remote Control

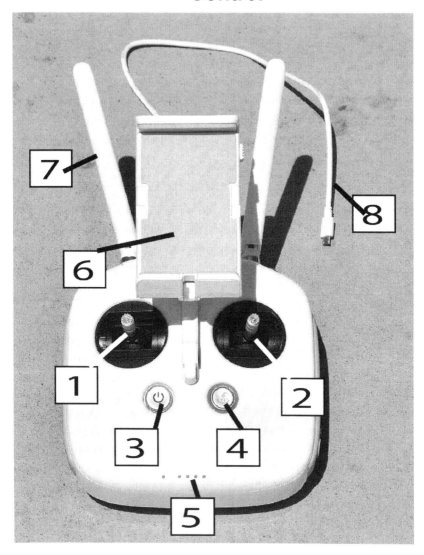

This is the remote control that came with the DJI Phantom 3 quadcopter. It looks a little different than the kit drone remote control doesn't it? It pretty much does the same thing. It just lacks all the customizable abilities.

1. This is the left flight stick.
2. This is the right flight stick.
3. This is the power button.
4. This is the RTH button.
5. These are status indicator lights that tell you the current status of the remote control and batteries.
6. This is a soft clamp that holds a tablet computer in place on top of the controller. You might be wondering what that is all about. With this model, you can plug in an Android or Apple tablet and get all sorts of great information about your current flight. You can see a live video feed from the camera. You can see pretty much all the status information you need like GPS signal, location on a map, altitude, speed, percentage of battery left and all of your camera functions. Once you try flying like this, you will never go back!
7. This is one of two antennas.
8. USB cable for attaching your tablet and getting all of that great information.

There are a few other buttons or switches located on the shoulders of this controller that operate camera functions and flight types. Another thing to note is the fact that the battery is part of the controller. It can't be taken out of the controller. If the battery fails for any reason, the entire controller must be replaced.

While each controller is indeed very different from each other, they both serve the same basic functions. The kit drone controller gives you more freedom and flexibility but is more difficult to program. The RTF controller gives you fewer options but is easier to get started.

It's time to look at the different drone brand names that are currently on the market.

Brand Names

If you haven't already started looking over the various drone manufacturers on the market, then you will quickly learn that there are quite a few of them actively competing for your business. These manufacturers want your money and they are creating new ideas, innovations and better features that make flying drones so much fun. All of this competition is great for you and me. It means we get more options, more choices and more ways to fly our drones.

You might have also noticed that drones can range in price from as little as $20 (£13.00) to as much as $10,000 (£6531.00) and everywhere in between. The cost of the drone should play a major factor in whether or not you decide to buy. Look over all of the features and extras you might need before making your decision.

Is One Brand of Drone Better Than Another?
Some people would say, "Yes! This brand is much better than that brand!" That's fine, but the best drone is the drone that delivers exactly what you want it to at a price you can afford. You might not need a drone that has a high definition 4k camera attached to a 3-axis gimbal. You might prefer something with less features.

You might even notice that some people get a little upset if you don't like a particular drone brand and that's just fine too because at the end of the day all that matters is what you think. Does your drone give you everything you expected it to? If it does, then good for you. If it does not, then you might want to start investigating alternatives.

Here are a few of the more popular consumer RTF and kit drone manufacturers on the market as of this writing. The technology associated with these drones is changing every single day so there may be some new manufacturers on the market that I haven't had a chance to list in this book.

3DR Flying Machines

3DR or 3D Robotics has a large line of drones available on the market. Their rather impressive lineup consists of several very different flying machines that cover a wide range of prices and options. From the hobbyist to commercial applications, 3DR offers a drone for everyone. To see their full line of products, visit their website:

http://3drobotics.com/

Their latest offering in the hobbyist market is causing quite a stir. It is called Solo. Solo is a RTF quadcopter that offers some very impressive features geared towards aerial photography. If you don't have an interest in aerial photography, then this might not be the drone for you.

Solo has the ability to get some serious Hollywood style movie production shots with just the touch of a button. You can take selfies, use the Solo like a cablecam, have the Solo fly around you in circles using Orbit mode and you can tell the Solo to follow you where ever you go. These are great features that every photographer and aerial video enthusiast is looking for, but the Solo offers even more on top of these great features which include:

- LED lights for directional awareness
- Powerful onboard computer system
- Powerful motors
- Accessory bay
- Intelligent controller
- An optional 3-axis gimbal

The 3DR Solo does not come with its own camera. You will have to bring your own camera in order to harness the full potential of this flying machine. In fact, all of these great features were created specifically for the GoPro line of HD cameras. This can be good or bad.

You can expect around 20 minutes of flight time on one fully charged battery with the Solo.

If you already happen to own a GoPro camera, then you are one step ahead. If you don't already own one, then you are looking at spending more money to get started.

3DR is somewhat of a newcomer to the consumer hobby drone market, but they offer up an unbeatable warranty that states: "If the flight logs show Solo was lost or damaged due to a system error, 3DR will immediately repair or replace not only the drone, but your gimbal and GoPro® as well."

Blade Flying Machines

Blade offers quite a few RTF drones for the consumer hobbyist. From the smaller and less expensive nanodrones to a larger quad with a built in high definition camera, Blade offers a drone for just about anyone.

Their entry level nanodrones are less than $100 (£65.00) and are the perfect choice for anyone who wants to see what its like to fly a drone. The small price tag on the Blade nanocopters makes it a very attractive flying machine.

When you are ready to move up to something with a little more power or a drone with a camera, you will find quite a few good choices. The Blade Chroma is the perfect example. It features four different drones within the same product line. This gives you more choices and more bang for your buck.

The four models include:

CGO3: 4K -1080P 16 MP camera, 3-axis gimbal, remote control with touch screen display, telemetry information and live video feed, 30 minute flight time, battery, charger and multiple flight modes.

CGO2: 1080P 16 MP camera, 3-axis gimbal, remote control with touch screen display, telemetry information and live video feed, 30 minute flight time, battery, charger and multiple flight modes.

GPH4: This model is made specifically for GoPro cameras. It features 3-axis gimbal, remote control with touch screen display, telemetry information and live video feed, 30 minute flight time, battery, charger and multiple flight modes. This is a good choice if you already own a GoPro.

BNF: This model is made specifically for GoPro cameras but does not feature a 3-axis gimbal. It comes with a fixed mount. If you are looking for stunning aerial photography, then don't even bother with this model.

Other features include: remote control with touch screen display, telemetry information and live video feed, 30 minute flight time, battery, charger and multiple flight modes. This is a good choice if you already own a GoPro.

DJI Flying Machines

DJI is undoubtedly the consumer drone king. There are more DJI flying machines out there in the world today than any other manufacturer. There are several reasons for this. DJI offers several excellent RTF drones and some of the best industry leading kit drones. By doing this, DJI has the market pretty well covered.

With all that said, DJI drones might not be the perfect choice for your first flying machine. While the RTF models are easy enough to use, they do come with a small learning curve. However, DJI drones do make an excellent choice for when you are ready to take off your training wheel and do some real flying.

DJI Kit Drones
The DJI kit drones come in a couple of models. You can choose a quad or hexcopter and put the entire thing together just like I did. Just make sure you put the right props on the right motors. You will be required to use your own camera with these kit models.

DJI RTF Drones
DJI offers plenty of RTF models as well. At the time of this writing there were three Phantom models. Each varying in price as well as features.

Phantom 1: The Phantom 1 was the first mass market consumer quad offered by DJI. Its entry level price will get you up in the air, but you will need to bring your own GoPro camera if you want to take any type of video or pictures from the air.

Phantom 2: The Phantom 2 comes in three models. The basic Phantom 2 is an excellent little flying machine with no camera.

The Phantom 2 Vision includes a built in HD camera and the first integrated FPV flying experience.

The Phantom 2 Vision+ includes a stabilized high definition video camera as well. All of the Phantom 2 flying machines work as advertised.

Phantom 3: At the time of this writing, the Phantom 3 was the latest offering from DJI and it comes in two models. The Professional and the Advanced. The professional model features a 4k 12MP camera with a 3-axis gimbal. The Advanced features a 1080P camera with a 3-axis gimbal.

Both models feature FPV through an attached tablet or smartphone and both models are good choices for a serious aerial photography drone.

DJI Inspire

DJI also offers a more professional level aerial photography drone called the Inspire. This professional drone has all the bells and whistles you would expect from a professional level aerial photography drone. You can also expect a larger price tag to come along with it.

Flight time varies from 8 minutes to as long as 24 minutes on some models.

DJI also offers a large line professional aerial photography drones called Spreading Wings. These are big drones capable of carrying the heavier DSLR cameras. These are for the serious photographer who is planning in making some money with aerial photography and video. Price tags on these models start at around $1900 (£1239) and go as high as $4500 (£2935).

Overall, DJI makes an excellent drone for anyone who is ready to take their flying skills to the next level. Be sure to visit their website for more details. Www.dji.com

GoPro Flying Machines

At the time of this writing, GoPro has not released a consumer drone just yet. They have talked briefly about their plans for releasing a drone that puts their cameras in the air. They have mentioned using virtual reality technology with their offering but no specs have been revealed yet.

You can bet the GoPro drone will be worth every penny. GoPro knows what they are doing when it comes to capturing great high definition footage, but the competition does have a huge head start!

Hubsan Flying Machines

If you are looking for some good entry level flying machines, then Hubsan might be the right choice for you. They offer some very affordable nanodrones that will get you more than prepared for flying some of the big boy machines.

The lower cost of these machines makes them very popular for people who are thinking about getting started in the addictive world of flying drones. For less than $50.00 (£32.00) you can get your hands on a small, easy to fly nanocopter and slowly work your way up from there.

They offer models with small cameras that will let you take photographs and record video and they also offer a model with a HD camera and gimbal. The model that features the HD camera is the Hubsan X4 PRO and it boasts a flying time of 40 minutes.

The Hubsan X4 Pro also has several other great features that include: GPS, Automatic Return, Compass, Automatic take off and landing, FPV and something not currently found on other models. The X4 Pro has a safety parachute that deploys during collisions. This helps return the drone safely to the ground instead of breaking into several pieces. This is a great innovation that is sure to make its way into other consumer drones on the market.

For more information visit the Hubsan website: http://www.hubsan.com/

Parrot Flying Machines

Parrot offers several drones for the consumer hobbyist. You will find small nanodrones that are perfect for learning the ropes, and you will also find some entry level drones with cameras and FPV capabilities.

Their flagship model is called the Parrot Bebop and its price tag puts it right in the middle of the camera drone market. The Parrot Bebop was designed with safety in mind and it can be flown using nothing more than a Android powered smart phone or an Apple iPhone using the free Freeflight 3 app. The controls appear right on the screen. This means there is just one less thing to bring with you.

The included HD 14 MP camera shoots 1080P video at 30 FPS. The flight time is around 22 minutes with two batteries.

If you don't want to spend a lot of money on a consumer drone that takes decent photos and video, then the Bebop might be the right choice for you. You can find more information on their website.

http://www.parrot.com/usa/products/bebop-drone/

Syma Flying Machines

Syma is also an excellent brand to start with because they offer everything from small reasonably priced RTF nanocopters to larger RTF quadcopters with built in cameras and everything in between. The first two nanodrones I purchased were made by Syma and I have no complaints.

If you are looking for something a little larger with a camera attached to it, then you will also find plenty under the Syma brand.

X11C Air-Cam : An entry level quadcopter with a small HD camera attached to it. Don't expect anything amazing in terms of picture or video quality, but this model is a great way to start seeing what things look like from the sky. You can expect a flight time of 6-8 minutes.

X5C Explorers : A slight step up from the X11C, this model features a small HD cam that will allow you to see the world from the sky. Flight time is around 7 minutes for the particular model.

Overall the Syma line of drones is geared towards the beginner who just wants to see what it is like to fly through the sky. Don't expect anything great in terms of video or picture quality either. This doesn't mean that you can't enjoy flying them though because they are a ton of fun.

To see the full Syma product line visit their website.

http://www.symatoys.com/

Yuneec Flying Machines

Yuneec drones are geared towards the photographer. Each one of their drones offers up some impressive features for anyone who is thinking about getting into aerial photography. Let's take a closer look at their entry level photography drone, the Q500 Typhoon.

Q500 Typhoon: Capture 1080P video at 60 frames per second with the Q500 Typhoon. This is a RTF model with everything you need to start capturing high definition aerial footage. The 12 megapixel camera is mounted to a 3-axis gimbal for smooth video every time your record.

You can also enjoy the FPV experience because the Q500 Typhoon has a live video feed built into the remote controller.

Don't forget the internal compass and GPS antenna for easy smooth flights. You can expect around 25 minutes of flight time. At the time of this writing, the Q500 Typhoon had an elevation limit of 8000 feet. If you plan on flying this machine from higher mountain areas, you might want to double check to see if this limitation is still in place.

Q500 Typhoon 4k: As you can tell by the name, this model features a high resolution 4k camera. The 12 megapixel camera captures 4k video at 30 frames per second or 1080P at 120 frames per second. You also get control over white balance and light exposure as well. The included 3-axis gimbal will ensure steady footage at all times.

Multiple flight modes make the Q500 Typhoon 4k a great video capture machine and the entire experience is sent back to a small monitor that is built into the controller for a great FPV experience.

The Q500 Typhoon 4k goes one step further for the video and photography enthusiast. You can detach the 4k camera and attach it to a hand held gimbal for recording great 4k video footage without the drone.

Tornado H920: This is a professional drone for professional aerial photography. At the time of this writing, the Tornado H920 was not available. It boasts a larger more powerful camera that is geared for professional aerial photographers.

For more information on the Yuneec product line visit their

website.

http://www.yuneec.com/

Where Should You Buy Your Drone?

Unfortunately there is a lot of counterfeiting in the drone market. There are fakes out there that might only give you one or two flights before falling from the sky like a rock. The single best way to avoid these counterfeit drones is to purchase from a reputable dealer you know and trust. This could be a local hobby shop or an online retailer.

Should You Buy Direct?
Some drone manufacturers also allow direct orders through their company websites. Just be cautious of what country the drone is actually shipping from. If the drone is coming from a country other than your own, then you might be expected to pay duty and large shipping charges. The same idea applies to shipping the drone back if it arrives in pieces. Pay close attention to where the drone is shipping from and where you are required to send it in if it needs repairs.

Online Retailers
You can find almost every single drone manufacturer I have listed on Amazon.com. Amazon has excellent customer service and they take good care of their

customers. If you run into a problem, you can bet Amazon will be there to help.

There are a few other online retailers worth mentioning as well. Like I said previously, just make sure you know which country their products are shipping from.

www.getfpv.com

www.readymaderc.com

www.hobbyking.com

www.helipal.com

http://www.quadcopters.co.uk/

You can also find some really good deals on Ebay as well. Just pay close attention to which country the drone is shipping from!

Be Careful of New Models

Drones are technology based flying machines. A lot of these technologies are still in their infancy and determining how well they actually work in real world scenarios is not something you should have to take part in, but unfortunately it happens.

Don't Be A Beta Tester!
Drone manufacturers have been known to release new models with just a few basic flight functions. There have also been RTF releases that did not work right out of the box. You can expect this type of problem with any new emerging technologies and manufacturers have no problems letting the public beta test their supposed finished products.

There is nothing wrong with holding off on your purchase until the manufacturer has managed to work out all or at least most of the kinks. There are a few other good reasons for not being the first person on the block to own the latest and greatest drone.

Waiting Saves Money!
As soon as a drone manufacturer announces a new product, prices on the earlier models drop every so slightly. If you can hold off until the newer drone is released to the public, then you will see prices dip down even further.

They say patience is a virtue and if you can wait long enough in the drone world, you can save a lot of time, frustration and money.

If you happen to get hooked on flying and you want to slowly build your own personal army of drones, waiting is also an excellent way to achieve total drone domination! Muw ha ha!

Short Supply
Brand new drones will also be in short supply. Some orders have been put on the dreaded back order list for far too long. Yet another excellent reason to wait until supply can meet the demand.

Not only will the drones themselves be in short supply but you can bet spare parts and accessories will be in short supply too. There most likely won't be any accessories on the market until a few months after the latest model is launched.

If you simply have to have the latest and greatest newest drone on the market, don't say I didn't warn you!

Accessories & Spare Parts

Depending on which drone you choose, you might not get everything you need to enjoy hours of constant enjoyable flight time. You may find out that you need some accessories in order to fully enjoy your new drone army.

Once you start digging in, you will see that there are all kinds of accessories depending on the model you chose. You will also notice that there are far more accessories for kit drones as opposed to RTF drones.

The drone is just the beginning, you will also be wanting or needing a few accessories. Here are some accessories I highly recommend considering.

Props

Your drone might have come with a few spare props and there is good reason for this. Props are easily the weakest part of the entire drone and they are usually the first part of the drone to come into impact with foreign objects. Trees, bushes, and grass are often the first objects to hit a prop and the prop almost never survives the impact.

Don't worry though because spare props don't usually have a large price tag unless of course you choose to buy some of the more expensive glass filled or carbon fiber props that are available as aftermarket accessories.

Prop Guards

The motors on these flying machines are spinning at a very high rate of speed. For example, the motors on the popular DJI phantom quadcopters spin an average of 7000rpm while hovering.

Accelerating or take off increases these speeds. Having one of these spinning props hit a finger could be very problematic. I don't know about you, but I like owning all of my fingers. Prop guards could help prevent a very serious accident. They could also prevent your drone from losing a prop due to a mid-air collision.

Landing Gear

Not all consumer drones come with what you can actually call Landing gear, but for the models that do come equipped with landing gear, it is often the second most likely piece that gets broken.

Hard landings are extremely common when you are learning how to fly your new machine. All it takes is one hard landing to snap your landing gear. You may or may not still be able to fly after an event like this. Owning a spare set of landing gear is a wise choice.

Batteries

Owning more than one battery is a must if you plan on

getting any amount of decent flight time out of your new drone, but not every drone on the market has a removable battery pack.

If the drone you have chosen does have a removable battery, then you will need at least one spare battery pack. Many avid pilots will have an entire stock pile of the things. I'm talking 10-20 additional batteries. This may seem a little overboard, but remember that you are only going to get in the neighborhood of 10-20 minutes per flight depending on the model and its payload.

Believe me when I tell you 10-20 minutes flies by (no pun intended) extremely fast when you are piloting your drone through the skies. Having more than one battery will ensure you get your fill of flying.

Sure, you can always recharge your single battery before flying again, but depending on the battery you might be looking at 1-2 hours charging time. Sometimes even longer. Buy at least one spare battery. You will thank me later.

Battery Voltage Tester
Some of the newer batteries on the market have built in LED status lights to tell you how much juice is left in the current charge. If you happened to buy a kit drone, then your batteries might not have this luxury.

You can find a Lipo Battery Voltage Tester Low Voltage Buzzer Alarm on Amazon. This will tell you what the current voltage is for your battery. You can also have this as a permanent part of your drone so you know when the battery level is low while flying.

Extra Battery Charger

If you are finding it difficult to wait for your batteries to charge, then luckily you can speed things up by purchasing an additional charger. With an additional charger you can charge both batteries at once. This is a great convenience.

Car Charger

You may also find that your basic home charger isn't enough either. How are you supposed to charge your additional batteries when you are miles from home? You could use an expensive inverter / generator or you could just buy a charger that either plugs into your vehicle's lighter or attaches directly to your car's battery.

Backpack

If you are anything like me, then you plan on taking your cool little flying machine to some far off places to get a bird's eye view of the world around you. It is easy enough to load all of your gear into your favorite driving vehicle, but what happens if you want to launch from an area that requires a hike?

That's where the backpack comes in really handy. There are several backpacks on the market that will allow you to safely transport your flying machine on your back. You can even use some of these to bring your flying machine with you on an airplane as carry on luggage. A backpack makes long hikes into the great beyond so much easier.

Lens Covers

If your drone has a camera, there may or may not be a variety of lens covers to not only help protect your lens, but to also capture better video and images. You will have to do some searching to see what is available. You can find anything from simple lens covers to filters that will alter the way your new camera in the sky perceives the world around you.

Tool Box

You might want to grab a little plastic tool or tackle box while you are it. You will need some specialized tools if you are going the drone kit route and keeping these tools with while you are out flying around will make things much easier if you need to do any quick repairs.

Batteries – The Real Power Behind Your Flying Machine

These little flying machines depend on one thing for their power source and one thing only. It is not gas. The drones of today use batteries, extremely high powered batteries that were not available just a few short years ago.

In fact, without these batteries you would most likely not be flying a drone today. Unless of course there was some other type of alien power source on the market from the planet known as Keplar 12 in the Udranian system, but that is top secret information that hasn't been released to the public just yet.

The small electric motors that are responsible for generating enough thrust to launch your machine into the air demand a huge amount of power. The larger the motor, the more power. The more motors, the more power. Indeed, these are power hungry aerial vehicles.

The batteries that are responsible for creating this vast amount of power are called Lipo batteries. Lipo is short for lithium-ion polymer. That in itself sounds like some space age alien technology doesn't it?

It is some pretty impressive stuff and I beg you not to glaze over the information in this section of the book. It is very important. I'm talking not burning your house down important.

Lipo batteries are very dangerous. All of the power that gets stored in these batteries has to be managed properly in order to prevent them from going exothermic. Exothermic might be a new word in your vocabulary and I didn't include it in the learning the lingo section above. Sorry about that.

The simplest definition for the word exothermic is the release of heat. In the case of a Lipo battery, this release of heat means fire. Very hot, very powerful, very destructive fire. This is no joke. Without the proper care a lipo battery will catch on fire. Notice how I said "will" not "if." These things are no joking matter, but you can't fly a decent drone without one or two of them. At least not yet.

If you choose to ignore this warning for any reason, you very well may end up seriously hurt. You have been warned. You might be saying to yourself, "I've handled plenty of NiCad or NiMH batteries in my day. I know what I am doing." Lipo batteries are very, very different. These are not your run of the mill batteries that can be bought at your local department store.

Proper Lipo Battery Care
You will need two very important things in order to

properly care for your Lipo batteries. You will need a Lipo charging bag. This bag is designed to contain a fire in the unfortunate case your lipo battery goes exothermic. You can find these bags at any hobby store and you can also find them on Amazon. Here is what mine looks like.

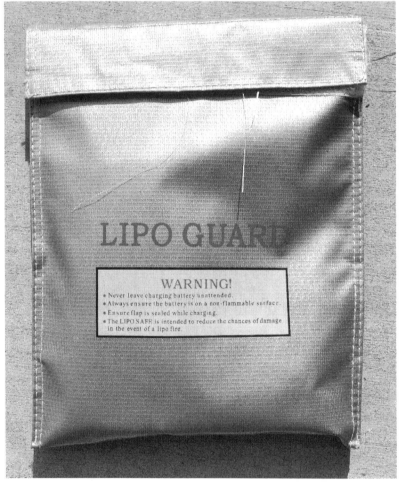

Use the Correct Charger

The next extremely important thing is the correct charger. Not every battery charger on the market can safely charge a lipo battery. Do not use a NiCad or NiMH battery charger to charge your lipo batteries. Only use a battery charger that has been designed to specifically charge lipo batteries.

With that being said, there are plenty of great chargers on the market that will charge all three types of batteries, but you have to make 100% sure that your charger has indeed been designed to charge lipo batteries. Charging your lipo batteries is the single most dangerous part of using them. Once again, you have been warned.

Balance and Cell Count

When charging your lipo batteries you have to pay very close attention to the cell count. Charging at the incorrect cell count will cause multiple problems for you and your battery. Read the instruction manual that came with your charger in order to determine how to set the cell count on the charger.

If your charger does not have a balance charge mode, then get a new charger. If each cell of your battery pack is not balanced properly (if each cell has a different voltage) then your battery pack could very well explode while you are charging it. A balance charge prevents this problem.

Don't be rushed into a fast charge either. Charging your lipo batteries on a slow balanced charge is the best way to not only prevent potential problems from occurring but it will also give you the longest battery life. When I say battery life, I don't mean flight times either. When I say battery life, I mean the overall lifespan of your battery. Your lipo batteries should last years with the proper care, charging, discharging and storage procedures.

Keep Your Eyes On Your Batteries While Charging
Never under any circumstances leave your lipo batteries unattended while they are charging. It doesn't matter if you have followed all of the proper charging procedures to the T.

The best way to prevent a fire from spreading is to be there when it starts. Yes, waiting for your lipo batteries to charge is about as much fun as watching paint dry, but you have got to stick around just in case there is a problem.

It's also a really good idea to charge your lipo batteries in an open area. If they do catch fire, then being in an open area will help keep any nasty fumes that get expelled when the battery catches fire from hurting anyone.

Fire Safe Charging Area
You should always charge your batteries in a fire safe area. This will help prevent the fire from spreading in the

unfortunate event that the battery does go exothermic. What exactly is a fire safe charging area you ask?

- A fire place
- Fire safes with vents
- Pyrex containers with sand in them
- Large concrete slabs with no flammable objects nearby
- Nuclear holocaust bunker in the backyard

These are just a few fire safe charging areas. The lipo bag I mentioned should be enough, but you can never go too far when it comes to fire safety.

What Should You Do If There Is A Fire?
Sand is the cheapest and safest way to extinguish a lipo battery fire. If you have followed all of the prior suggestions, then you should already be in a nice large open area where there is practically no chance of the fire spreading. Dumping a bucket of sand on the burning battery will suffocate the battery and prevent the fire from getting worse.

Bad Battery Symptoms
A bad lipo battery will display a couple common symptoms. The most obvious symptom is a bloated battery pack. One or more of the cells inside the pack might swell. You may feel the urge to pop or puncture the battery pack.

Do not under any circumstances do this.

If your lipo battery swells or bloats, very carefully remove it from the charger (if it was connected) and submerge it in a tub of salt water for two weeks. You can make your own salt water solution by mixing ½ cup of salt per one gallon of water.

After the battery has had a nice saltwater bath for two weeks you can remove it from the salt water, wrap it in newspaper and put it in the garbage. Unlike alkaline, NiCad and NiMH lipo batteries can be disposed of in landfills.

Crashes and Batteries
There is a good chance your battery could be damaged during a crash and the bad part is the battery may show no symptoms at all. If your drone does crash, very carefully inspect the battery pack. If there are any signs of damage carefully place the battery pack in a lipo bag or other fire safe container for at least two hours. After two hours, the lipo battery must be discharged using the right charger.

Discharging Your Batteries for Storage
In most cases your lipo batteries will be discharged while you are busy flying around the sky, but if you crashed your drone in mid-flight and you need to discharge your batteries, then use a charger that has a proper discharge

mode. Most lipo chargers have a built in discharge mode that makes this safe and easy.

If you are not planning on flying your drone for a few days, then you should discharge your batteries for storage and place them in a fire safe container. Once again, this is where the storage or discharge mode of your battery charger comes into play. Use it wisely.

If you happened to purchase a RTF drone, then this information may or may not pertain to you. Just make sure you read through the entire manual that came with your RTF drone before you attempt flying or charging your batteries.

Tools

If you are planning on going the kit drone route, then you will need some some what specialized tools in order to assemble your flying machine. If you are planning on buying a RTF drone, then you might still want to consider owning some of these tools. You never know when you may need to attempt a repair, and the following tools will come in really handy.

Torx Wrench Set
You will definitely need a really good torx wrench set and when I say "really good," I mean that literally. Most of the

screws that you will be dealing with are torx screws and most of them will be tiny.

I went through two torx wrenches before I figured this out. There are some really good torx wrenches on the market out there and there are even more really bad ones that are made from soft, brittle metal.

The tips of my first torx wrench stripped out on the second use. The second one I hastily picked up at the local electronics store where the helpful sales associate assured me the slightly expensive torx wrench set I had in my hands was made from hardened steel lasted through 4-5 screws.

Now I am nowhere near a huge muscle bound dude. In fact, I was very careful working with the torx screws because I did not want to strip them out. I barely tightened these things. I quickly returned the second set of torx wrenches and decided to locate some that would stand up to my needs.

I found a good set on Amazon that is nice and strong. I have been using them for a very long time and never had any issues.

Page 81

Here is a link to the set on Amazon.

http://www.amazon.com/gp/product/B002QV0FGA

If you are in another country other than the USA, the link above will not work, but don't worry because I have you covered.

Look for a torx set that features hardened steel. The ones I purchased stated the following:

- High quality chrome-vanadium-molybdenum steel, through hardened
- Black finish and through hardened for extreme durability

Look for something similar and make sure your set includes the following sizes at minimum:

- T6
- T7
- T8
- T9
- T10

Those five sizes should cover torx screws your may be

dealing with during assembly or repairs.

Soldering Iron
If you are going the kit route, then a decent soldering iron will be required as well. I recommend you get a 60 watt iron. You might be able to get away with a 30 or 40 watt iron, but a 60 watt will work much better.

Plastic Zip Ties
These little things will help you in more ways than one. I used quite a few of them to keep cables nice and tidy and temporarily affix components on my kit drone. They are lightweight, cost effective and easy enough to add or remove at any time.

If you plan on using plastic zip ties, you will also need a good set of wire clippers to cut off the excess pieces or remove one all together.

VHB Tape
Very strong, very sticky double sided tape will also come in very handy when you are putting your drone together or if you need to make some quick repairs. This stuff is lightweight and strong. These are two traits every piece of your drone should feature.

You can find vhb tape on Amazon or just Google "vhb tape."

What To Do When You Crash

Hopefully you never do actually crash, but the more flight time you get, the more likely you are to experience a crash. Crashes happen. Unfortunately they are part of the drone game. Your flying skills will play a huge part in preventing a crash, but even the pros crash their drones.

When you are dealing with several electrical components all bundled into a machine that flies great distances and soars high into the sky, you will eventually experience a crash. There are mechanical and electrical malfunctions that will quickly interrupt your peaceful day of flying and send your drone crashing to the ground. So what do you do when that fateful day comes?

Don't Panic!
This is easier said than done when you just watched your thousand dollar bird come crashing to the ground. Hopefully you didn't fly the drone away from your line of sight. You are technically supposed to keep visual contact with your little flying machine at all times. If you do maintain visual contact at all times, it will be much easier to recover the bird when it crashes.

If you didn't do this and decided to see how far you could fly your drone, then you might be out of luck unless of course you affixed a small GPS tracking device to your drone. If you did, then it is time to get tracking.

Your first instinct might be to go running through the hillside in search of your fallen drone. While this sounds like the perfect reaction, try to keep your wits about you. This is especially true if you are out on some mountain peak somewhere. Recovering your crashed drone is not worth losing your life. Take a few deep breathes and then head out looking.

Don't Power Off Your Controller!
If you did crash your drone and your drone survived the crash, then you still might be able to get some very useful information from it. It still might be broadcasting a live video feed to your controller. You might be able to use this live video feed to help you locate the drone. This is especially true if your drone managed to land somewhere high in a tree. You might be able to walk in front of the FPV camera and see yourself on the FPV display.

Some RTF and kit drones also feature some pretty comprehensive GPS features that allow you to see where your drone is on a digital map. Your drone might still be transmitting this data back to your controller. You might be able to use this information to lead you right to the crash site!

If your crash was really bad and your controller is not

displaying any GPS or FPV data, then you are going to have to do things the hard way. You will need to find your drone. This will be an almost impossible task if you flew your drone beyond your line of sight. Just another reason why you should not be doing this.

Once you are at the crash site, it will be time to pick up the pieces and determine the extent of the damage. Check out your batteries first. If they look okay, then you should power everything up to determine what works and what doesn't. You might be one of the lucky ones whose drone survived the crash with no damage. If so, consider yourself very lucky.

If your drone isn't working properly, then it is obviously time to pick up the pieces and head back home and do some repairs.

With all this being said, there are pilots who have flown their drones for years without ever experiencing a crash. You might be wondering how they manage to pull off such an incredible feat.

If you invested a lot of money in your drone, then you might be really be interested in finding out how you could fly it for years without ever experiencing a crash. The next two chapters are for you!

Practice Makes Perfect

When it comes to flying your little eye in the sky, practice really does make perfect. Knowing exactly what each button, knob and stick on your controller does makes things a whole lot easier.

Being able to fly your drone and understanding the different modes of flight will also go a very long way towards preventing a crash. I will cover the modes of flight in just a little bit. For now, let's talk about getting some flying hours under your wing before you actually fly your drone.

Flight Simulators

There are flight simulators on the market that have been specifically designed to help you learn how to fly your new drone, but it can be a little tricky getting a flight simulator to work with every drone model on the planet. Not to mention the fact that not all remote controllers are supported by all of the flight simulators on the market.

The most popular flight simulator is called AeroSIM and it can be found at www.aerosim.com. Make sure you look over their website and make sure your remote controller model is compatible with their software.

Using a program like this will help you get better

acquainted with your flying machine, but nothing will prepare you for real world challenges like the real world itself. When you start flying in the real world you have a whole mess of uncontrollable variables that come into play.

You have wind, elevations, altitudes, temperatures, weather, birds, trees and power lines just to name a few. No amount of flight simulator practice is going to help you deal with these potential problems simply because they can't be simulated! So where does that leave you?

I have already said this, but I am going to say it again. Take you drone out into a wide open space far away from any possible obstacle and start flying. Take baby steps and don't fly very far away. Get really comfortable with the controls and then slowly but surely start flying further away but remember to always keep your drone in sight!

Flying With Training Wheels or Assisted Flight Modes
I have already talked quite a bit about all of the wonderful technology that resides inside these little flying machines. Most of this technology is there for one simple reason. It is there to make flying your new drone easy. You could think of this technology as training wheels, or better yet, training wings. Well that doesn't really work either because these things don't have wings. Let's just say the technology makes flying easier, way easier. In fact, the only time you

should even attempt to fly without the technology is NEVER and here's why.

The GPS, compass, accelerometer, gyroscopes and flight controllers are all working really hard deep inside your drone. When they are all activated or working properly your new drone will hover perfectly in the air awaiting your commands.

All of this wonderful technology is what's making this happen. All kinds of crazy mathematical computations and mind boggling algorithms are being done in order to make flying easy, stable and intuitive.

Slight stick adjustments will change the flight path, speed or altitude. Small wind gusts don't even seem to bother the drone. It magically maintains stability and hovers effortlessly. You could think of this as the ZEN of flying. Simple, easy and very entertaining. If your drone has all of these great features, then you will be saying to yourself, "Flying this thing is easy!"

Trying to fly a drone without any assistance from this technology or in complete manual flight mode is a much different story. Without it, your drone would be much more difficult to fly. It will not hover and it will not maneuver very easily. Even the slightest wind will make your drone drift and lose or gain altitude. It will appear as if your easy to fly drone is a totally different machine. It will not be easy to fly!

Common Flight Modes and What They Mean

Even though there are several different drone manufacturers pushing their little flying machines into the consumer market, they all share some common flight modes. In order to make one product sound better than the next, manufacturers might even use some different terminology to describe these flight modes even though they are the same.

Here are the three most common modes of flight listed from the most difficult to the easy, breezy, drinking a beer with one hand and eating some potato chips with the other while you fly your drone with your big toe easy.

Manual Mode – With manual mode there is nothing helping you fly your drone. You are it. This is the most difficult flying mode and it is only recommended for highly experienced pilots.

Now there is nothing wrong with taking your drone to some far away place where there are no obstacles and giving good old manual flight mode a try. There may be a day when some of the technology inside your drone stops working. Guess what flight mode you will be using if this happens? Manual mode. It doesn't hurt to know how your drone will respond in manual mode, but only try this in big open spaces far from any people, places or things.

Attitude Mode – In Attitude mode there is only one thing helping you keep your drone stable and it doesn't help all that much. Flying in attitude mode is far easier than flying in full out manual mode, but you will still find the wind pushing your drone this way and that.

Like manual mode, only attempt this in a big open space. It will help you learn how your drone responds if it loses GPS signal.

GPS Mode – This is that magical flight mode that you should be using. This is the one where all that great technology makes flying super easy. Of course this mode of flight only works when and if your drone has the ability to lock onto multiple GPS satellites.

Rules or Laws

Yes, there are rules, regulations, ordinances and laws in place that may or may not govern where, how and why you can fly your fancy new drone. These rules have been put in place in an attempt to make flying safer for all of us and because some people have been doing less than intelligent things with their drones.

There has been more than one occasion where a person has crashed their fun little flying machine on the White House lawn and people have used their camera equipped drones to spy on their neighbors.

Because of these people who seem to lack something we call "common sense," it is becoming more and more difficult to find a legal place to actually fly your drone. If you want to be a responsible pilot and prevent any additional flight restrictive rules for every other responsible drone pilot out there, then make sure you follow the current rules.

Current Drone Flying Laws In the USA
The FAA or Federal Aviation Administration is the sole American agency responsible for policing our skies. These are the people who make the rules. They lay down the law. The FAA determines where, when, how and why you can fly. If you don't happen to be in the USA, then there is

probably some sort of agency in your home country that is responsible for the same type of thing. It is your responsibility as a drone pilot to make sure you are following the current rules.

At the time of this writing, these were the current drone flying rules put in place by the FAA. DO NOT SKIP THIS SECTION.

National Parks Are Off Limits

You are not allowed to fly a drone in any national park in the United States. Doing so will get your drone confiscated and you will most likely be fined. I hate to be the one to tell you but that epic aerial footage you wanted of the Grand Canyon won't be happening.

You can thank the countless idiots who have flown their drones in national parks and done very stupid things with them. Yes, people have crashed their drones into Old Faithful at Yellowstone National Park and because of their stupidity, no one is allowed to fly a drone in a national park. You will quickly see that many of the current drone rules are in place because of all the idiotic things people have done with their drones.

Hobby or Recreational Drone Flying

If you are flying your drone just for the sheer fun and thrill of flying, then there are a few things to keep in mind at all times when you are flying. These rules change from location to location. For instance, your local city might have an ordinance in place that prevents you from flying your eye in the sky. It is up to you to determine if there is such an ordinance in place.

The general rules for flying your drone are pretty much common sense but the excitement of flying can often bury common sense somewhere deep in your subconscious so try to remember these flying basics any time you launch your flying machine into the sky.

Do not fly around large groups of people or over any people for that matter. If for some reason your drone comes falling from the sky, you don't want to be the one responsible for injuring someone.

- Do not fly at altitudes greater than 400 feet (121 meters) and believe me 400 feet in the sky is way up there. If you go higher than that, then you will not be able to see your drone. At 200 feet (60 meters) up, the drone is a mere dot in the sky. This will also prevent you from crashing your drone into any type of commercial aircraft which are typically not allowed to fly below 500 feet (152 meters.) That leaves a nice 100 foot (30 meter) cushion between your drone and commercial aircraft.
- Never fly your drone beyond your line of sight! This

means you should have visual contact with your drone at all times. If you need a helper to help you keep your eyes on your drone at all times, then use one. You might have a nice FPV video connection showing you what the drone sees, but what happens if you are depending on that live video feed and it stops working? You might not get your drone back.

- Do not fly over vehicles, and stay at least 25 feet from property susceptible to damage.
- Do not fly within a five mile (8 kilometer) radius of an airport.
- Do not fly in bad weather. This includes high winds, rain or fog.
- Do not fly your drone over areas like prisons (yes it has been done), power stations, dams, busy roadways, water treatment plants and government buildings. Flying in these areas is just asking for serious trouble.
- Do not fly your drone after you have been drinking or taking any type of drugs. This includes prescription medicines!
- Do not fly over private property. It is private for a reason and you should respect that.
- Do not use your drone to spy on your neighbors, your ex-girlfriend, your ex-boyfriend, your ex-whatever or anyone else for that matter. This means you should not be capturing video footage, images

or peeking in on any person without their consent. This is a really good way to get your drone smashed and your butt kicked.

Using Your Drone Commercially

If you want to use your drone to make money by taking aerial photographs, shooting video, or abducting small farm animals, then you need an FAA Airworthiness certificate. What is an FAA Airworthiness certificate? It is basically a pilot's license. So in order to use your drone commercially in the USA, you will need a pilot's license. Obtaining a pilot's license is not going to be easy and it will cost a good chunk of change.

There is an exemption process in place known as the "Section 333 Exemption." This exemption is approved on a case by case basis but most of the exemptions still require some sort of pilot's license.

There have been plenty of businesses who have been granted a Section 333 Exemption and in the fine print of the exemption, it states the need for a pilot's license. It is being speculated that many of the people flying their drones for commercial purposes under the Section 333 Exemption don't have any type of pilot's license, but this is just speculation.

In the mean time, the FAA is busy creating a new set of

rules for people who want to fly their drones commercially. Here is a summary of their proposed rules:

- Unmanned aircraft must weigh less than 55 lbs. (25 kg). Operational Limitations
- Visual line-of-sight (VLOS) only; the unmanned aircraft must remain within VLOS of the operator or visual observer at all times the small unmanned aircraft must remain close enough to the operator for the operator to be capable of seeing the aircraft with vision unaided by any device other than corrective lenses.
- Small unmanned aircraft may not operate over any persons not directly involved in the operation.
- Daylight-only operations (official sunrise to official sunset, local time).
- Must yield right-of-way to other aircraft, manned or unmanned.
- May use visual observer (VO) but not required.
- First-person view camera cannot satisfy "see-and-avoid" requirement but can be used as long as requirement is satisfied in other ways.
- Maximum airspeed of 100 mph (87 knots).
- Maximum altitude of 500 feet above ground level.
- Minimum weather visibility of 3 miles from control station.
- No operations are allowed in Class A (18,000 feet &

above) airspace.
- Operations in Class B, C, D and E airspace are allowed with the required ATC permission.
- Operations in Class G airspace are allowed without ATC permission.
- No person may act as an operator or VO for more than one unmanned aircraft operation at one time.
- No careless or reckless operations.
- Requires preflight inspection by the operator.
- A person may not operate a small unmanned aircraft if he or she knows or has reason to know of any physical or mental condition that would interfere with the safe operation of a small UAS.
- Proposes a microUAS option that would allow operations in Class G airspace, over people not involved in the operation, provided the operator certifies he or she has the requisite aeronautical knowledge to perform the operation.

Pilots of a small UAS would be considered "operators". Operator Certification and Responsibilities include:
- Operators would be required to: Pass an initial aeronautical knowledge test at an FAA-approved knowledge testing center.
- Be vetted by the Transportation Security Administration.
- Obtain an unmanned aircraft operator certificate

with a small UAS rating (like existing pilot airman certificates, never expires).

- Pass a recurrent aeronautical knowledge test every 24 months.
- Be at least 17 years old.
- Make available to the FAA, upon request, the small UAS for inspection or testing, and any associated documents/records required to be kept under the proposed rule.
- Report an accident to the FAA within 10 days of any operation that results in injury or property damage.
- Conduct a preflight inspection, to include specific aircraft and control station systems checks, to ensure the small UAS is safe for operation.
- FAA airworthiness certification not required. However, operator must maintain a small UAS in condition for safe operation and prior to flight must inspect the UAS to ensure that it is in a condition for safe operation. Aircraft Registration required (same requirements that apply to all other aircraft).

Aircraft markings required (same requirements that apply to all other aircraft). If aircraft is too small to display markings in standard size, then the aircraft simply needs to display markings in the largest practicable manner.

Model Aircraft: Proposed rule would not apply to model aircraft that satisfy all of the criteria specified in Section 336 of Public Law 112-95.

The proposed rule would codify the FAA's enforcement authority in part 101 by prohibiting model aircraft operators from endangering the safety of the NAS.

At the time of this writing, these were the proposed rules. They were not the rules that have been put into the law books yet.

No Fly Zones

There are places in the United states where you are not supposed to fly your drone. If you read the previous chapter, then you should already know this. Knowing where you can and can not legally fly your new drone will save you a lot of trouble.

Thankfully we have this great technology at our disposal known as the Internet. There are a few great websites complete with interactive maps showing you where you can and where you can't fly in the United States. It would be a really good idea to familiarize yourself with these websites before you fly.

https://www.mapbox.com/drone/no-fly/

http://www.dji.com/fly-safe/category-mc

If you are a property owner and you would like to add your property to the drone no fly zone, (Just think of this as the do not call list for drone flights.) then visit this website and add your property address to the database.

https://www.noflyzone.org/

Preflight Safety Routines

If you read the rules or laws section completely, and you should have because you are a responsible pilot right? Just nod your head yes. You might have noticed a preflight inspection was mentioned quite a few times.

Not only is this a great idea for safety reasons, but it could also prevent you from losing your fancy flying camera. Some of the items listed in this preflight checklist might not pertain to your specific drone model. This is a generic preflight safety routine guide. Use what applies to you and your drone.

Surroundings Checklist
Before you attempt flying be aware of your surroundings. This means you should be aware of everything in your flight zone. Common things people overlook that cause huge problems are:

- trees
- people
- power lines
- buildings
- bodies of water
- airports

Take a very good look around and make sure there are no obstacles. Be aware of everything!

Hardware Checklist
You are one step closer to being a responsible drone pilot. Time to make sure you have everything you need to fly.

- Drone
- Drone power source. In this case a battery or batteries.
- Remote control
- Camera
- Sd Card if your drone is equipped with a camera.

Preflight Hardware Inspection
Before you fly, it is a really good idea to take a very close look at every single part of your drone. All of these should be done before powering up your drone.

- Inspect all props for anything unusual like cracks or

uneven surfaces. Make sure they are on good and tight too! Nothing brings a drone down faster than a busted prop. Well, a direct hit with a shotgun blast might bring it down quicker, but let's hope you don't run into that sort of problem.

- Inspect the drone body for any type of damage. Look over the arms, landing gear and body. Look for cracks, loose screws or loose wires.
- Check all connections and make sure all plugs and connections are firmly seated.
- Check all batteries for damage and correct charge levels.
- Make sure all batteries are firmly in place. I bet you can imagine what happens if your battery becomes disconnected in mid-flight. You can say bye bye to your drone.
- Make sure all sticks on your remote control are centered.
- Make sure your drone has a good GPS signal and is locked onto multiple satellites if it has the ability to do so.
- Make sure home position is set and locked as well before liftoff!

If everything looks good, you are ready to start up the motors! Refer to the instructions that came with your drone for instructions on how to start up the motors. It is usually a combination flight stick movement. Here is how I start the motors on my drones.

Pull both sticks down at the same time and then move them into the left corners like the image below.

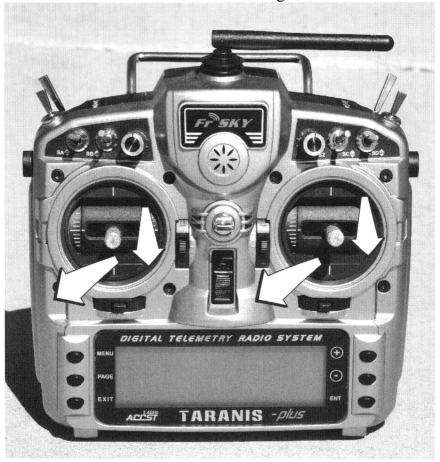

The DJI Phantom uses the same idea but a different stick

pattern in order to start the motors. You pull both flight sticks down at the same time and then move them both towards the center like the image below.

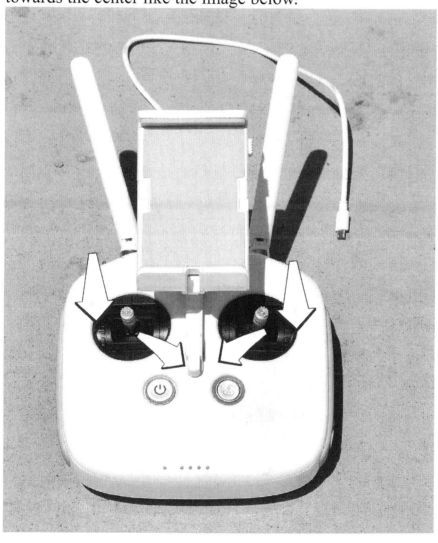

Understanding the Basic Controls

The time has finally arrived. You get to pilot your fancy little flying machine. You might have already taken it for a test spin or two. Either way, it is an exciting moment and knowing exactly what every little stick, knob, switch or button on your remote control does will help immensely. Let's take a closer look at how you will be controlling your drone!

Flight or Control Sticks
The majority of controllers use two flight sticks to steer your drone through the sky. They are simply labeled, right and left. Pretty simple and basic stuff.

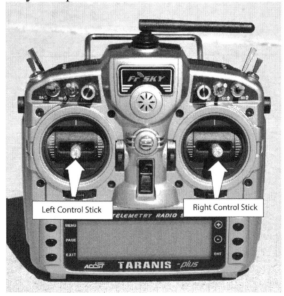

Mode I vs Mode II

There are two common controller modes found in today's drone remote controls. They are labeled, "Mode I" and "Mode II." The majority of the people in the United States fly in Mode II.

In Mode II, the left stick controls the thrust, altitude and yaw and the right stick controls speed, side to side movement and forward and reverse movements. Don't worry, I will give you some pictures and illustrations in just a minute that make it easier to understand what's going to happen when you move each flight stick.

In Mode I, the flight sticks are reversed. The right stick controls height, side to side movement and forward and reverse movements. The left stick controls forward and backwards movement and yaw.

Wouldn't it be nice if there was some standard control scheme that everyone used? Yes it would. Well, there's not. Sorry about that. I didn't design this stuff but I will make it easier to understand, and in order to makes things easier and less confusing, I am only going to cover MODE II. This is the most popular flight stick control pattern.

Mode II (United States Flying) Left Stick Explained

The left stick has two functions. The first function is

getting your drone off the ground. Slowly pressing up on the left stick will slowly lift your drone into the air.

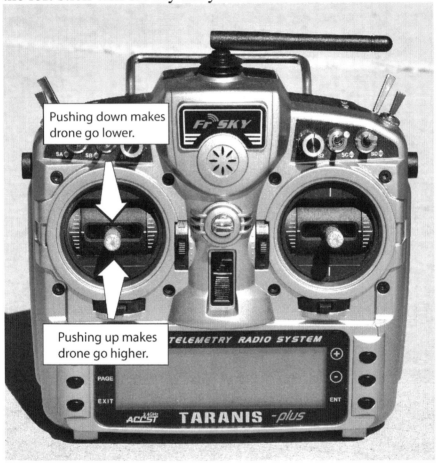

Pushing down makes drone go lower.

Pushing up makes drone go higher.

Now, This next section depends on the drone model you are currently flying. If you let go of the left stick and it returns to the center position, your drone should hover at its current altitude. All of the fancy internal technology is what makes it hover and stay in position.

If you want your drone to go higher, gently push the left stick up. If you want to bring your drone back to earth, gently press the left stick down. A word of warning to you. Never descend quickly. Your drone will experience something known as Vortex Ring State and it will most likely crash. I will explain Vortex Ring State in detail in a later chapter but for now, just remember to descend nice and slowly.

That's it! You now know how to fly your drone. Go forth and fly! Of course, I am kidding here. You haven't even learned the half of it yet!

I mentioned the left stick having two primary flight functions. Here is the other function and this only works while your drone is airborne.

Pressing the left stick to the left will make your drone rotate to the left or counterclockwise but only if the front of the drone is facing away from you. If the front of the drone is facing you, then pushing left on the left stick will rotate your drone to the right or clockwise.

Keep in mind this stick movement on its own will only rotate the drone around its own center of gravity. This is a great way to get a nice panoramic view of the world around you. See image below.

Front of drone

Pushing the left stick to the left will make the drone rotate counter clockwise.

Pushing the left stick to the right will make your drone rotate to the right or clockwise.

This movement also depends on which direction the front of the drone is facing. See the images below.

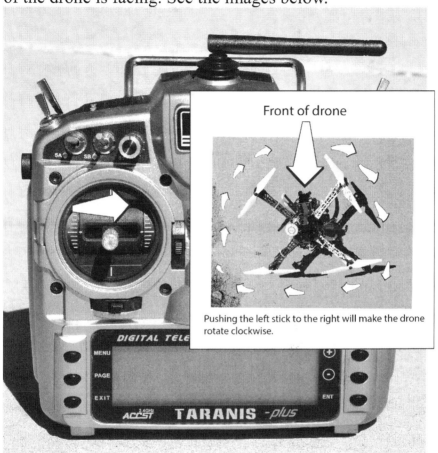

Front of drone

Pushing the left stick to the right will make the drone rotate clockwise.

Mode II (United States Flying) Right Stick Explained

The right stick also has two flight functions and they also only work while your drone is in the air. If you press the right stick up, the nose or front of the drone will dip down and the entire drone will move forward. If you press the right stick down, the nose or front of the drone will dip upwards and the drone will move backwards. See the images below.

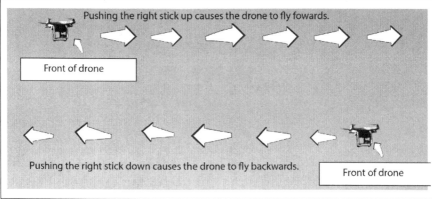

Pushing the right stick up causes the drone to fly fowards.

Front of drone

Pushing the right stick down causes the drone to fly backwards.

Front of drone

The right stick also has another function. If you press the right stick to the left, the drone will move to the left. If you press the right stick to the right, the drone will move to the right. See the images below.

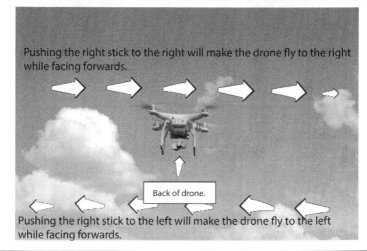

Pushing the right stick to the right will make the drone fly to the right while facing forwards.

Back of drone.

Pushing the right stick to the left will make the drone fly to the left while facing forwards.

If you press the right stick to the upper right corner, your drone will move forward and right at the same time at an angle. If your press the right stick to the upper left corner, your drone will fly forwards and to the left at an angle.

If you press the right stick down to the bottom right corner, your drone will fly backwards and to the right. If you press the right stick down to the bottom left corner, your drone will fly backwards and to the left.

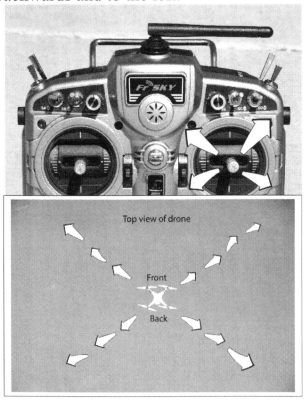

Notice how the left stick wasn't used for these maneuvers? The internal technology should have been keeping your drone level at its current altitude. If your drone isn't equipped with any of those fancy things, then you would be required to maintain a steady altitude by pushing the left stick up or down. This would only be the case in some of the less expensive models.

Those are the basic flight stick operations when used on their own. Let's take a look at some more advanced combination flight stick movements.

Advanced Combination Flight Stick Controls

Are you ready to learn how to fly your drone better than a peregrine and break the sound barrier? If you answered yes to that question, then you need to join the Air Force because you are going to get that kind of control out of these consumer hobby drones, but you can learn a few great flying techniques that are fun and great for filming!

Forward Ascent
One of the easiest flying techniques to master is the forward ascent. Your little flying machine will fly forward and go higher at the same exact time.

Pulling this off is really simple. You slowly press the left stick up until your drone is at a good starting altitude. This could be a couple of feet (1 meter) or more from the ground. Once you have the perfect starting altitude, slowly push the right stick forward and the left stick forward at the same time like the image below.

Front of drone

If you do this correctly, your drone should fly forward and up at the same time.

Forward Descent
The forward descent is just as easy to master. Once your drone has reached a good altitude, slowly press the left stick forward and the right stick down at the same time. Look at the image below.

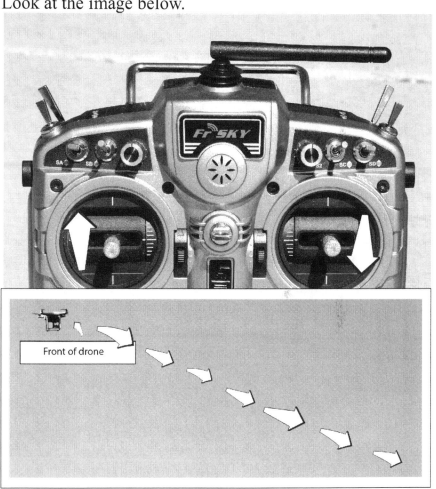

Front of drone

Your drone should slowly move forward and lose altitude at the same time. You can do the same thing and make your drone fly in reverse as well. Just slowly pull both sticks down at the same time. This is the safest way to land your drone and using this method flight maneuver will eliminate the Vortex Ring State. I will explain this in an upcoming chapter.

Just remember that your controls will be backwards if your drone is flying towards you. Pushing the right stick to the right will make the drone go left. Pushing the right stick to the left will make the drone go towards the right.

If you practice these two very basic flight stick controls, you will get a better feel for how your drone flies.

Flying In Circles Around An Object
This can be one of the most difficult maneuvers to master, but with a little practice it gets easy. This is a great maneuver for filming.

Suppose you want to fly your drone in a counterclockwise pattern around something while keeping the nose or camera pointed at the object in the center at all times. You would slowly push the left stick to the left while pushing the right stick up and to the right diagonally like the image below.

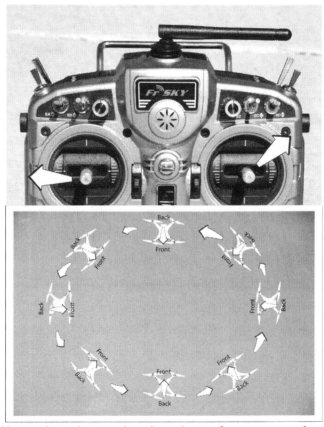

You will need to determine just how far you need to push

each stick in order to determine the pattern radius and speed at which the drone moves across this radius. It can be tricky to master.

If you wanted to move your drone in the opposite or a clockwise pattern while keeping the nose or camera pointed at an object, then you would slowly press the left stick towards the right while pushing the right stick up and to the left diagonally like the image below.

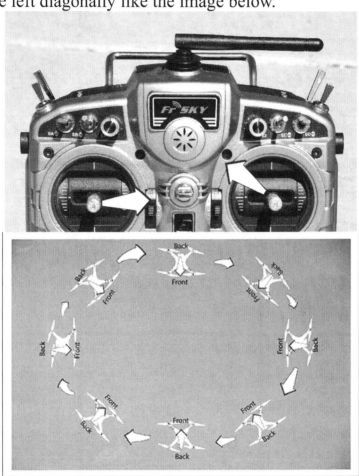

There you have it! You now know some of the more basic and difficult flight stick patterns that will pilot your drone to new heights. Congratulations. You are almost ready to go forth and fly, but you need to know a little more about the best and worst times to fly; Vortex Ring State and how to avoid this almost guaranteed way to crash your drone.

The Best and Worst Times To Fly

Now that you know all those simple and somewhat fancy ways to pilot your drone you may be wondering if there are "good" times to fly and "bad" times to fly. There are. The best times to fly are in the early morning or later in the afternoon.

Now this could very well be 100% dependent on your current location. I choose to fly at these times for various reasons. The weather is almost always near perfect early in the morning.

Strong winds will make it difficult to fly your drone. You should avoid any flying during gusty or even moderate wind speed changes. The weather is usually nice and calm early in the morning. The same goes for later in the afternoon as well. The weather is more cooperative at these times.

I also choose to fly at these times because they offer the

best photo and video opportunities. Flying in the middle of the day is fun but the sun can ruin your photos and videos. I talk a little more in detail about this in a later chapter.

Those couple of hours directly after the sun has risen and the couple of hours right before it sets offer the best color and light situations for capturing astounding video and breathtaking images.

What About the Worst Times to Fly?

Just like there are "good" times to fly, there are also "bad" times to fly as well. It has to do with the whole duality, yin and yang thing. Light, dark. Good, evil. Best times to fly. Worst times to fly.

You should not fly your drone during adverse weather conditions. This means stormy weather. Unless of course you want to be the first person to pilot a drone into the middle of a tornado in hopes of capturing insane footage that helps the scientific community get a better understanding of what the inside of a tornado looks like. I think there was a Hollywood movie based on something like this but they didn't use drones.

Great, I have just given all the storm chasers the greatest idea in the world. I think I deserve a cut of their proceeds. You can find my email address at the end of the book. Feel free to email me royalties.

You know that you shouldn't be flying your drone in bad weather. Wind, rain and lighting will quickly bring your bird down, but are there any other conditions where you should avoid flying? I'm glad you asked. Yes, there are.

If you have one of the more fancy drones that uses GPS and all of those other technological advances, then it would be wise to pay close attention to solar flares. The sun can render the GPS inside your drone practically useless and flying will become very difficult to say the least.

Luckily there is a website that will tell you when these types of solar events are happening.

http://www.swpc.noaa.gov/products/planetary-k-index

This type of information will help you prevent all kinds of seemingly unpredictable flying problems from happening.

Time

Flying your drone is one of the rare situations when time is not on your side. You will have a somewhat small amount of time to safely fly your drone. You may also notice that you only get a few minutes of actual flight time from your batteries. It could be as little as 5 minutes or as long as 40. The total amount of time in the air will depend on a few things including your drone model, battery, weather conditions and elevation.

Keep Your Eyes On Your Flight Time!
Yet another thing you need to be aware of when you are busy flying, your flight time. Flying too long or too far away is a guaranteed way to crash. Some of the more fancy RTF drones will tell you how long you have been in the air with some sort of visual readout. This information may appear on your remote control or it could appear on some other type of viewing device.

If you don't have this luxury, then you need to manually keep track of how long you have been flying if you want to avoid running out of battery juice in mid-flight. There are a few simple ways to do this.

You could use a watch to time your flights. I know, I know, the concept of using a watch to track time is a little odd. You could also use your smart phone to help you keep track of time as well. You might even be one of those unique people who can glance at the sun and know exactly what time it is. You could then track the sun's movement to determine how long you have been flying.

Regardless of how you choose to track your flight times, you must do it in order to avoid a crash. It is far too easy to get excited while flying and lose track of time. Don't do this. Pay attention to your flight time and avoid one of the most common crash mistakes the average drone pilot makes.

Extending Flight Times

If you are anything like me, then you will want to learn how to extend your flight times. Those few short minutes of flying time never seem to last long enough. You know what they say, "Time flies when you are having fun!"

The easiest way to extend your flight times is by purchasing more batteries. Having more fully charged batteries on hand will give plenty more flying time. Most drone fliers will have at least three batteries at minimum. Some people have anywhere from 10-50 batteries. Yeah, I know. That's a lot of batteries.

A bigger battery with more power will get you more time in the air but it will also add a good bit of weight to your drone. The added weight could very well even out the added battery power. You will have to experiment with this idea and see what you can come up with.

Lose Some Weight
Another way to extend your flight time is by lowering the amount of weight you are carrying with you in the sky. This may not be possible on some models, but on others you may be able to remove the camera, the gimbal, prop guards or other smaller pieces in order to get more time in the air. It doesn't take much either. Being able to remove a few grams of weight can give you a few extra minutes. A lighter drone will have more flying time.

Better Props
You might also be able to extend your flight times by getting better props. The stock props that come with most drones can be changed. Larger props can give you more flying time but not too much.

With the larger props you will also lose some maneuverability as well. It is a trade off and you might be fine with losing maneuverability in exchange for an additional minute or two in the air.

Buy Another Drone!
Two drones is always better than one and having another one on hand will double your flying time. Having a second

drone is also a good idea because you will have a backup drone to fly just in case you crash your first one!

Vortex Ring State or Settling With Power

Like most new drone pilots, the idea of landing and the landing approach is almost always the same. You slowly approach the landing zone and then descend straight down. There is nothing wrong with landing your drone this way as long as you do not descend too quickly. If you do, then you might encounter Vortex Ring State.

Vortex Ring State happens when your drone descends into its own downwash. Downwash is a term for the air that is being forced down by your props. The props on your drone are creating a powerful wall of downward flowing air. This wall of air flow is what lifts your drone into the sky.

When you descend too quickly, your drone gets caught in this powerful wall of downward flowing air. This force of air will push your drone to the ground very quickly. It will almost appear as if it is free falling. It may also randomly start rolling or pitching from side to side.

Getting things under control once the Vortex Ring State has fully developed can be next to impossible. If you can catch the Vortex Ring State before it fully develops, you might have a chance at gaining control of your drone.

The initial reaction is to try and fly your drone up. This would be a huge mistake because by flying up you are essentially increasing power. Increasing power adds more downward air force making the Vortex Ring State worse. Your drone will fall faster than a brick made from solid gold.

To recover, you must move your drone forward, backwards or sideways. You have to get your drone out of the downwash and you have to do it quickly. Piloting your drone forward, backwards or sideways will help you get your drone out of the prop downwash.

Worse case scenario? Your drone flips in mid air and falls to the ground in pieces and hopefully doesn't injure anyone below.

Avoiding the Vortex Ring State
The easiest way to avoid the Vortex Ring State is to slowly descend at an angle like the image on the next page.

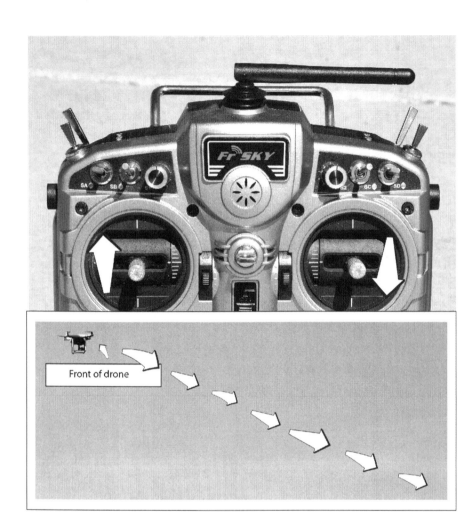

This type of landing might take a little more space. If you are short on space just descend at an angle as much as you can, stop and hover, turn your drone around and start your angled descent in the other direction. This is the easiest way to avoid this problem.

If you choose to fly your drone up really high and then choose to fly it straight down, you will most likely crash. You have been warned.

Capturing Great Video and Tack Sharp Images

The next chapter is devoted entirely to drones with cameras which is a huge percentage of today's market. If you want to capture breathtaking videos and totally awesome still images with your drone, then you will need a couple of things.

Of course you will need a decent camera. The higher resolution or the higher mega pixel the better. That means you will need a camera capable of capturing high definition video in a variety of resolutions and an adjustable field of view.

Your on board camera should be able to capture video in 720P at minimum if you want anything worth looking at. 1080P is preferred and 4K is currently the best. That doesn't leave you with many really good options. Luckily, most drones have a built in camera and those that don't can be equipped with the widely popular GoPro camera.

You will also need a drone that is equipped with a gimbal. You can capture video footage with a drone that doesn't have a gimbal but the footage won't be worth looking at. It will be too jumpy and shaky to watch.

Camera Settings

How you setup your camera will have a huge impact on the quality of footage you capture. The first thing that needs to be addressed is the field of view. Some of the newer DJI Phantom drones have this portion under control already and you won't need to mess with any settings.

If you are using a GoPro, don't use the SUPERWIDE or WIDE. Try to stick with the MEDIUM field of view setting. This will prevent that fisheye look which can be somewhat of a bother in aerial footage.

Fly Smooth and Easy

The best footage comes from nice steady flying. Crazy and erratic aerial movements will capture crazy and unusable video footage. The same goes for still images. I prefer to stop in place and hover when I take my still shots. I also avoid fast rotating movements for aerial video as well. It is disorienting and ruins the footage.

Let the drone's forward or backwards movement capture the video. Trying slowly panning down with your camera while ascending but only pan your camera about half way down. This makes for some really impressive cinematic footage. I often sit in wonder at the footage I have captured. It looks like a National Geographic documentary.

Hey, if you are a big wig at National Geographic looking for some awesome aerial footage shoot me an email. I might be able to help you out. Of course, not commercially because that is currently against the law in the United States.

Flying your drone at a downward angle while slowly panning your camera up will also make for some really nice views. Just remember to fly nice and easy and your footage should be mind blowing. There is nothing quite like seeing the world around you from the vantage point of your drone. It can be incredible in the right situations.

There is another important reason to fly nice and easy while your are capturing video. If you move your drone forward too quickly, the front of the drone dips down a few degrees and as a result you will see props in the top of your video. This is a quick way to ruin a great shot.

If you must fly your drone quickly while capturing footage, try doing it backwards. The front of your drone will tilt up instead of down and you won't get props in your video. Yes your footage will be flying backwards but you can just reverse the footage when you are editing. Now you have perfect, fast forward flying footage.

It can be a little tricky trying to accurately fly your drone and capture great footage at the same time. It takes practice and focusing on capturing great footage can be a great way to crash. Don't get too involved in your footage. Remember to keep an eye on your drone while it is in the sky.

Some of the more advanced drones on the market come with two remote controls. This makes it easy to fly and film with two pilots. One person pilots the drone, the other handles all of the camera work.

Oh Know There's Jello!
Kids seem to love Jello. I never was a fan of the stuff. Something about the way it just sat there wiggling and undulating on my plate made me always say, "No thanks." I am definitely not a fan of Jello when it comes to flying drones either. You might be saying to yourself, "What the heck is this guy talking about?"

Jello is a common problem that appears in high definition drone footage. The footage appears a little rubbery in places, like it is made from jello. The real problem is the fact that you can't really see the Jello effect while you are busy flying your drone. You are flying and capturing that world class footage and when you get home and preview it on the big screen, the footage looks rubbery.

You may also notice that the jello effect only seems to happen when the sun is at its brightest. That is your first clue.

Your gimbal is supposed to make the jello effect disappear, but it doesn't always work. The only way to completely eliminate this nasty video artifact is to use a neutral density filter on the drone's camera.

A neutral density filter is like sunglasses for the camera on your drone. It helps block out some of that really harsh sunlight that is making the jello effect appear. Using a neutral density filter will allow you to use a slower shutter speed and completely eliminate the jello effect. Of course this trick is only helpful if the camera in your drone let's you adjust the shutter speed.

For instance, the camera on my Phantom 3 drone let's me change the shutter speed. On a very bright sunny day, I have to choose a fast shutter speed of around 1/1000th of a second to keep the colors in the video footage looking good and to prevent the video from being overexposed. Overexposed video looks too bright and washed out. It is ugly.

If I slow down the shutter speed, I let more light into the camera. This will overexpose the image. The neutral density filter allows me to block some of the light which in turn let's me choose a slower shutter speed of around $1/100^{th}$ of a second. The end result is exceptional video footage that is not overexposed and most importantly gets rid of that nasty looking jello effect.

Getting Rid of Prop Shadows
You may have noticed the occasional horizontal dark shadowy looking lines in your video as well. This happens when you fly towards the sun. Just like the jello effect, this is being caused by too much light entering the camera. Can you guess how you would get rid of this problem? If you guessed a neutral density filter, then you are 100% correct.

This completes your video / photography lesson for the day! Now go out there and fly! While you are at it, capture some truly breathtaking video using the tips I just gave you and share it with the world.

Join the Community

Believe it or not, there are millions of other people out there who are also interested in flying some type of model aircraft. It could be a gas powered airplane that moves at insanely quick speeds or it could be a drone exactly like the one you currently own. Luckily for all of us there are quite a few great places where all of us can get together and talk about things like: extending flight times, preventing crashes and other really valuable tips.

If you want to make contact with other people who also have an interest in flying around the skies using planes, quads and drones, then you might want to join a local RC model club. Finding a local club is easy and the best place to start is the Academy of Model Aeronautics.

http://www.modelaircraft.org/

They even provide a really useful club search tool located here:

http://www.modelaircraft.org/clubsearch.aspx

If you can't manage to find a local club using their handy search feature, then you might want to try searching on your own. Just use the Internet to search for the largest city closest to you along with the words "rc flight club."

For instance: if you live in Boulder, Colorado; search for "Boulder rc flight club" without the quotes. You might be surprised by the amount of results you get.

There are quite a few people who have been involved in the hobby of flying model aircraft for years. Joining one of these clubs is the single best way to connect with them and learn from them as well. The more you know about flying, the less likely you are to experience a crash.

Online Communities

You don't have to join a local club because the Internet has made connecting with people all over the world so much easier and guess what? There are dozens of online communities full of eager pilots who are more than happy to share their knowledge.

The great thing about these online communities is the fact that they are highly specialized to specific types of flying. In this case, you can find online communities that are dedicated specifically to flying drones just like yours.

These online communities can be a great source of information when and if you have a problem. The other great thing about these online communities is this. You don't even have to participate if you don't want to. You can just read and absorb as much information as possible. Although it would benefit everyone if you contribute some information as well.

http://forum.dji.com/ - This is an excellent resource for the very popular line of DJI drones. You can find a section dedicated to every model they currently make from the insanely popular Phantom series to the Kit drones they offer. A great source of information for DJI pilots.

http://www.phantompilots.com/ - Another excellent forum

dedicated to DJI Phantom pilots.

http://droneflyers.com/talk/ - Nice little forum that covers a wide variety of drone models and pilots.

http://diydrones.com/forum – This forum is dedicated to those of us who like to take the DIY approach. Just about everything is covered from aerial photography to building your own drone.

http://www.hobbyking.com/hobbyking/forum/forum_topic s.asp?FID=94 – This forum is run by one of the largest online RC stores.

http://quadcopterforum.com/ - Dedicated specifically to quadcopters.

http://www.rcgroups.com/aircraft-electric-multirotors-790/ - Tons of great info on remote control helicopters.

http://www.rcdiscuss.com/forumdisplay.php?159 – Dedicated to all things drone.

http://multirotorforums.com/forums/ar-drone-forum.10/ - Dedicated to the popular line of AR drones.

http://forum.parrot.com/ardrone/en/ - Dedicated to the popular line of Parrot Ar Drones.

http://www.ardrone-flyers.com/forum/ - Another great resource dedicated to the popular AR drones.

https://www.skypixel.com/ - This community is a little different and if you aren't hooked on the idea of Aerial photography, then you will be after you look over this online aerial photography and cinematography community. This forum is run by DJI, makers of the very popular Phantom line of drones.

Thanks!

Thanks a lot for reading through my book. If you enjoyed reading, then feel free to leave a review. I would really appreciate it.

Learning how to fly your new drone takes a little time. I have given you everything you need to know on how to safely pilot your drone through the skies. If you have any questions, comments, concerns or if you would like to share some of your great aerial videos and images by all means, email me at the following address:

wordsaremything@gmail.com

I would love to hear from you. Have fun out there!
Mark Smith

P.S.

I am currently in the process of writing several more great drone related books. If you want to be the first to find out about any new books that I publish and how you can get your own free copy, then sign up to my **new book release** email list.

I promise not to share your email address with anyone, and I won't send you tons of junk mail. (I will only contact you when a new book comes out.) Follow this link.

http://eepurl.com/brgiXn

More Books By the Author

When Mark isn't busy researching and writing books, he loves to spend time outside enjoying the world around him and participating in a wide variety of outdoor hobbies. He loves to share his knowledge with the world and his best selling books have helped countless people get outside and enjoy our big blue planet.

His books have been praised by young and old alike for their ability to make things easier to understand. The laid back, conversational tone of Mark's writing style makes his books easy to read. His sense of humor keeps readers engaged and smiling. His excitement and passion for outdoor hobbies is highly addictive and many of his readers find themselves quickly wanting to join him for adventure. Enjoy some of Mark's other best selling books.

Metal Detecting: A Beginner's Guide: to Mastering the Greatest Hobby In the World

Incredible Metal Detecting Discoveries: True Stories of Amazing Treasures Found by Everyday People

Metal Detecting Gold: A Beginner's Guide to Modern Gold Prospecting

Coin Hunting Made Easy: Finding Silver, Gold and Other Rare Valuable Coins for Profit and Fun

Made in the USA
San Bernardino, CA
02 January 2016